W9-CUX-214

MONKEYSHINES ...& OTHER UNNATURAL ACTS

by: Vincent Palazzo

Theatrical Ink Press
New York • 1986

ISBN 0-937283-02-9

The Three Presses Agency
Leasing Department
39 Tompkins Street
Staten Island, New York 10304

Cover Illustration by: Powell Burns
Theatrical Ink Press logo by: Bill Starr
Author's photo by: Jeremy Sundgaard

TABLE OF CONTENTS

To some this may seem like an invention, but whatever I imagine to have happened did actually happen, *at least to me.*

—TROPIC OF CAPRICORN
Henry Miller

Curtain Raiser: **MONSTERS**

MONSTERS
a play without sound

In memory of Bill Vorenberg, a teacher, a director, a kind and gentle human being.

Cast:
A Derelict
Two School Children
A Young Girl
A Teacher

Place:
A clearing in a Manhattan park.

Time:
A Spring afternoon around lunch time.

Author's Note:
The roles of children should be played by adults dressed like kids.

(*A figure stands near center stage contained in a spotlight.*)

An elderly derelict remains virtually motionless staring towards the floor for long second. There is an apparent emptiness in his existence at this moment . . .

(*fade in. The scene is a small park situated near a grammar school.*)

The void passes quickly as a sound, unheard by the audience, snaps his head erect. The old man gazes intently into the audience for a long moment, then, shaking his head in disbelief, slowly turns around. His head again sags forward.

The sound unheard repeats again. The head snaps up. The derelict's arms extend slowly overhead. His hands bend inward taking on the appearance of claws. The transition continues and soon there is a hump on his back.

(*In an instant, the actions become intense . . .*)

The monster wheels about, dramatically returning to the audience. His face is contorted, grandly snarling a silent creature's language.

(*Two school children enter. They both appear to be no more than ten year old, dressed in the plaid uniforms of a private school.*)

They are obviously pleased by the monster, giggling, pointing and chattering with childlike delight. As the monster watches, his expression melts momentarily.

The old monster growls again with more relish than before. The children scurry in, then retreat as he begins to chase them playfully about the park. They never cease to speak in their own peculiar language. This is obviously a game enacted with ritual consistency.

(The Young Girl enters from behind and begins to stalk the monster.)

At the right moment, he wheels about in grand theatrical style and bellows over the Young Girl, who screams with delight and retreats. The two children now chase the monster as he hunts the Young Girl.
The game continues . . .

(The School Teacher enters. She is a stiffly attired stereotype of about thirty. She carries a gold bell.)

The Teacher stands firmly in place staring disdainfully at the monster.

After a pause, she waves her hand overhead permitting the gold bell to toll. The sound, again unheard, immediately catches the attention of the two children. They freeze. The old monster and the Young Girl continue the game. Each is oblivious to the sound.

The motion is repeated. Another sound is uttered. The Young Girl stops. The elderly creature is left with no recourse but to stare at the Teacher.

Majestically, with one stern point of her finger, the children are called before her. They move quickly and mechanically, forming a proper line in front of her.

Another majestic movement. The children march from view. For a long moment both the teacher and the monster watch each other. Then, with one final, disgusted contortion, she exits leaving him alone.

Facing the audience, the monster is again transformed, unravelling as it were, returning to his previous image. The old man is left on stage as the same feeling of emptiness again descends. He avoids looking at the audience.

(a pause)

The Young Girl re-enters with great reserve. She approaches the old man and places something in his hand. He does not notice until she has again left the park.

He looks at his palm and smiles, slowly raising his head erect. There is a piece of hard candy in his hand. The old man puts it in his mouth and smiles again.

The old man turns towards the exit. Looks. Nods. He returns to the audience. The Monster's face returns.

Growls . . .

(*fade slowly as the play ends.*)

One: **MONKEYSHINES**

MONKEYSHINES

This play is dedicated, with thanks, to Terrence McNally.

Cast:

Jeremy — 28; tall, lean and hairy; a lower echelon executive.

Gloria — a woman in her late twenties.

Place:

A room divided into two areas: the larger space is decorated in a Monkey House motif similar to those jungle scenes contained at the local zoo. A log balance beam and a swing are prominent. Vines hang from the ceiling. A jungle mural covers most of the rear wall. A small door is cut through the mural. Two large display boards, blank throughout much of the play, flank the cell. The smaller area contains a section of a simple, conventional living-room. A chair, an end table and a computer are prominent.

Time:

The present.

PROLOGUE

(Total darkness. And, total quiet.)
(Slowly, the sounds of a jungle become audible. Birds, insects and animals of all sizes are heard. The different voices grow slowly in intensity until . . .)

VOICE
Hello . . . are you still out there . . .

(silence)

Could you turn the lights back on . . .
Please . . .

(silence)

I'm sorry I yelled . . .

(An ape grunts. It is a little sound.)

It won't happen again . . .
I promise . . .

(another grunt—a little stronger.)

Please . . .
I'm sorry . . .

(More than one ape. The sound is almost like laughter.)

Please . . .

(The sounds fade slowly. The prologue ends.)

SCENE ONE

(*darkness*)
(*Slowly, dawn breaks over the jungle. A man, Jeremy, is sleeping on the floor. He is naked. A woman, Gloria, is in the living room observing the scene.*)
(*As the light grows more intense, Jeremy awakens with a start. He remembers where he is.*)

Author's note:
It should be understood that Gloria uses more than speech for communication. Her various tools include the sounds of the jungle, the din of the animals and the grunts and screams of the ape. She controls the general environment within the cage—with the help of a computer—and uses each to convey her purpose.

JEREMY

CHRIST!
(*pause*)
Hello . . .

(*The silence of the jungle breaks suddenly and the cell is alive with animal sounds—primarily screeching birds.*)

Shit! I don't know why you keep doing that. It doesn't help. I just want to talk. I know you're out there. I can here you. Why don't you answer? (*a little louder*) *Can't you hear me?* Is there a problem . . . something wrong with the sound system? Is that it? I'm not getting through. (*louder, animated*) LOOK AT ME. I-WANT-TO-TALK-WITH YOU.

Look! Read my lips! Talk to me! Do you understand what I'm . . . hey, can you see me? (*sarcastic*) If you can't, I've been walking around like a virgin boy scout on his first campout for no damn good reason. I didn't intend that to be funny—so, if you're laughing, please stop. I haven't felt this awkward in years.
(*pause*)

I think we should talk. Can you hear me?

(*The jungle noises stop abruptly*)

Thank you.

(*long pause*)

Are you still out there? I can't see a thing through this . . . this . . . whatever the hell this glass is.

(*another long pause*)

I'd like to get out of here. I don't mean to be rude . . . I don't want to upset your plans . . . hell, I don't even know what your plans are . . . but I'd like to leave. Hello!
(*grunting sounds*)

What do you want?

(*grunts and gorilla screams*)

Can we talk?

(*louder grunts and gorilla screams*)

Look! I don't like games. I never play them . . . not even when I'm home. I don't even own a deck of cards. (*slight pause*) I'm not enjoying this.

(*huge grunts and screams*)

Why are you doing this!

(*silence*)

(*A small door, large enough only for small objects, opens. There is a bright light inside which immediately gets his attention. Jeremy rushes to the door and discovers a bunch of bananas.*)

BANANAS!!
I don't *want* bananas!

(*the door closes*)

I just want to get out of here. Do you understand? OUT! AWAY! This isn't funny and I'm not playing . . . so you can forget whatever the hell it is you have in mind. *It's not going to work.*

(*the door opens. The bananas are gone.*)

Oh, dear god! Help me! Get me out of here!

(*Abrupt blackout*)

PLEASE!

SCENE TWO

(*lights up abruptly*)

JEREMY

Oh! Hello again . . .
I'm glad you're back. I've been thinking about you . . . trying to remember you . . . anything really. It's still pretty fuzzy . . . nothing makes much sense. I have this mental picture of a crowded bar. Lots of people but no faces. And, no noise. That's the strange part. No conversation. No music. Nothing. It's as if all the clues have been erased. It must have been some drunk. I'm sorry it ended.

GLORIA

(*matter-of-fact*) You only had one drink.

JEREMY

My god! You can talk! Thank you! (*pause*) Say that again.

GLORIA

You only had one drink.

JEREMY

That's great. I was beginning to think no one was really out there. Maybe now I can get some . . .

GLORIA

You only had *one* drink.

JEREMY

I'm not going to argue with you. I'm not the world's greatest drinker—I know that—so the drunk part doesn't surprise me. I do have a few questions about the rest of it though. (*slight pause*) Like: where am I, where are my clothes . . . why am I . . .

GLORIA

I took them off.

JEREMY

Oh!

GLORIA

You got sick on me.

JEREMY

I'm sorry. I don't remember. Where am I?

GLORIA

With me.

JEREMY

That's not what I mean. Where? What place is this? (*no response*) It must have been some party.

GLORIA

It was over right away.

JEREMY

Did I . . . we . . . eh . . .

GLORIA

Don't you remember?

JEREMY

No.

GLORIA

I was lucky.

JEREMY

Is that good?

GLORIA

For me.

JEREMY

This has never happened to me before.

GLORIA

I know.

JEREMY

I'm embarrassed.

GLORIA

No need . . .

JEREMY

But there is. I mean . . . I don't know who you are. I don't
even remember your name. I must have really tied one on.

GLORIA

You only had one drink.

JEREMY

Look . . . I told you . . . I get drunk now and then . . . and it
doesn't take much . . . I mean, I don't have to work at it . . .
but it always takes more than one.

GLORIA

Not this time.

JEREMY

A lot more for something like this. (*to himself*) Christ! If
this is a dream, I take the pledge.

GLORIA

Only one!

JEREMY

I don't believe that. I must have been drunk before we met.

GLORIA

Where?

JEREMY

If I knew that . . . I'd guess a bar. That's what you're getting at . . . isn't it? That's a clue. (*to himself*) Drinks . . .
drinks . . . that's it, isn't it? We were drinking . . . you and I
. . . in that nameless bar. That's it! *It was a pick-up!* This
whole thing . . . *this* started as a goddamn pick-up! *Jesus!* I
don't believe it. *I* started this!! What the hell did I ever see
in you!

(*screeching birds*)

No!! No, don't do that! Please! It was a mistake. I didn't
mean anything. *I'm sorry.*

(*screeching birds subside but remain audible.*)

It's just . . . well . . . I don't remember you. I don't have the
slightest idea what you want . . . or why you're doing this. I
mean, you went to a lot of trouble . . .

(*grunts*)

If I did something—believe me—it was unintentional.
What else can I say? What can I do?

(*louder grunts*)

Tell me . . . what do you want! *Tell me! Tell me, damn it!!*

(*loud grunts and screams*)

I'd like to see you.

(*abrupt silence*)

(*The door opens. There is a photograph inside. Jeremy studies it. And then* . . .)

Oh, Christ! I . . . I remember. I didn't do anything. Not a damn thing. You . . . you bought *me* a drink . . . you . . . one drink . . . and . . . and . . . you were there when I came in . . . and . . . you bought me a drink . . . and . . . and . . . I took it and laughed . . . I remember laughing and . . . and . . .

GLORIA

I took you home.

(*abrupt blackout*)

JEREMY

Why! *WHY!!* (*silence*)

SCENE THREE

JEREMY

I'd feel a lot better if I knew where I was. (*pause*) I mean . . .
am I in an apartment . . . a house . . . your home? Am I still
in the city? The country? This country? I assume you're
American. (*slight pause*) Are you? Am I still in *the* country?

GLORIA

It doesn't matter.

JEREMY

It does to me. I'd like to . . .

GLORIA

You *are* home.

JEREMY

I'd like to leave. (*no response*) I said, I'd like to leave.

GLORIA

(*matter-of-fact*) No.

JEREMY

Could I have my clothes?

GLORIA

No.

JEREMY

Please.

GLORIA

No.

JEREMY

Could you turn up the lights. I'd like to see you.

GLORIA

No.

JEREMY

NO! NO! NO! *Why the hell not!*

GLORIA

I like it dark. It pleases me.

JEREMY

I don't care. Do you hear me? I do not fuckin' care! I'm not comfortable in the dark. I want to see you. Turn on the damn lights!

(*Suddenly, painfully bright lights are turned on in the cage.*)

GLORIA

You are hardly in a position to order anything.

JEREMY

I've had enough. I'm leaving.

GLORIA

From where? Look around. There are no doors. No windows. No way in and certainly no way out. You are here to stay—permanently. I suggest you get used to the idea.

JEREMY

LET ME OUT OF HERE!!

GLORIA

Go to sleep. The party's over.

JEREMY

You're in a lot of trouble! I'll see to that. I'll see . . . I'll call the cops. I'll tell them everything. You think about that. Abuse. Kidnapping. The works. There are laws. Just you wait and see. There is a lot I can do.

GLORIA

(*very quiet*) And, there is a lot I can do. Think about that. And, while you're thinking, keep in mind . . . please keep in mind . . . that I . . . I alone . . . control everything that happens in there. *Everything* that happens to you, I allow to happen. I can take care of you . . . keep you happy . . . or I can do nothing. Think about that, too. In other words, I suggest you be nice . . . very, very nice . . . to this lady or she might . . . just might . . . decide to take a long . . . a very long . . . vacation very much alone.

JEREMY

Look . . . lady . . . I'm sorry . . . I'm . . .

(*blackout*)

Let me out of here . . . please

SCENE FOUR

(*It is very cold.*)

JEREMY

Could you turn up the heat . . . even just a little? I mean, I'm finding it very difficult to stay warm these days.

(*no response*)

I'd like to hear from you again. I still think it would help. I might even understand . . . I don't think I could accept this . . . but I might understand what you want. I could help . . . did you think of that? I could help. Work with you. Maybe speed things along. Think about it, okay?

(*sudden blackout*)

You know, this is ridiculous. I'm hungry. I'm cold. I'm naked and uncomfortable. And, I'm out with a woman I hardly remember. Just once, I'd like to date like ordinary people.

(*lights to normal*)

No offense . . . but . . . I mean . . . things like this don't happen to ordinary people. They don't worry about the people they meet in bars. It either feels right or it doesn't. It's simple . . . you know . . . for ordinary people.

If it's right, you spring for her drinks . . . maybe even the premium stock if you're feeling really good . . . and you talk. Casually. Nothing heavy . . . not for awhile, anyway. And, when you're ready . . . when the moments right . . . you suggest something—I don't know, maybe it's too crowded or you tell her the drinks are watered—and the two of you head somewhere a little more private and drink the good stuff. It's simple. (*shrugs*) And, if it doesn't feel right, it doesn't cost you much. You spend a couple of uncomfortable, unproductive, polite moments before excusing yourself. You can head to the men's room, I guess—to keep yourself honest—and a little while later you show up further down the bar . . . drink in hand.

(*slight pause*)

And that, dear lady, is the well rounded mating ritual of ordinary people. I guess I haven't had too much luck.

(*pause*)

Couldn't we talk . . . casually . . . for awhile.

GLORIA

No.

JEREMY

Damnit, lady! This isn't right. I mean . . . shit! Other guys go out and they drink—I mean they drink all night—and the worst they wake up with is a bad hangover. (*almost to himself*) Me . . . I have one drink . . . one stinkin' drink . . . and I wake up behind bars jailed by a fuckin' madwoman! This has got to be the greatest commercial ever written for alcoholics anonymous!

(*a pause as he gets control of himself*)

Look . . . I'm sorry. I mean it. I'm upset. Okay?

(*pause*)

I don't know what you have in mind . . . but . . . you know
. . . you've really got to know . . . it's not working. It's not
. . . well . . . right.

GLORIA

What I have in mind is a game . . . a time-honored, very
familiar ritual. We've already played the first part. If *it*
isn't *right,* my options will be very, very limited. Keep that
in mind.

(*silence*)

JEREMY

(*weakly*) Couldn't you just go to the men's room

(*abrupt blackout*)

Jesus!

SCENE FIVE

JEREMY

I've been thinking about what you said.

(*pause*)

Hello.

(*pause*)

I told you I didn't like games. That's not true . . . I'm just not good at them. The rules confuse me. I can't figure out what to do next—not until it's too late. I get involved when I shouldn't and probably miss out on the best of it by quitting too soon.

GLORIA

The rules change. It depends on who holds the dice.

JEREMY

I know. I don't want to play anymore.

GLORIA

You don't have a choice. The play is in motion. I began a long time ago . . . in that bar with our paid pieces of conversation and a few ounces of obligation. Those are the rules —your rules; the standard, tried and true, unrelenting rules. I accept them.

(*slight pause*)

I've paid for the drinks—and *I* hold the dice. Shall we talk "casually"?

                    JEREMY
I'm not going to play.

                    GLORIA
I see.

                    JEREMY
It's . . . wrong.

                    GLORIA
I can wait.

(*blackout*)

SCENE SIX

JEREMY

Have you thought about masturbation? I mean . . . lately. (*slight pause*) It's a subject tailor made to this situation. I mean . . . you've been very quiet lately. And I've been doing all the talking. I need something . . . some way of passing time from day to day . . . and masturbation seems a damn sight more interesting than solitaire.

(*an ape grunts*)

Does that interest you? (*he grunts*) I'm just trying to understand.

(*an ape grunts*)
(*Jeremy grunts back*)

We have to reach an understanding. I'm running out of things to say.

(*another grunt*)
(*Jeremy grunts back*)

Okay?

(*silence*)

I don't know why . . . I remember these friends . . . they'd call it *self abuse*. They were very polite, religious, college catholic boys. They'd never call it what it is—"jerking off". They'd never think of it. Hell, they'd never think to do it!

(*loud grunts*)

Well—guys—let me tell you something: jerking off is great! I mean, it's yours: the whole damn, ever-lovin' thing, from beginning to end, just runs through your head like some A-Number-One, fucking, first-rate, dirty, stag-type film festival starring your favorite, first choice, first person, pumping away, fucking away star! All color action! Humping! Bumping! Jumping! Licking! Sucking! Moaning! Groaning! *Super Stereo Sound!!* Cheap backroom, red light, down and dirty, sleazy bar music! Each frame, your frame your film . . .

Your fantasy. . .

Your fist. . .

Your FUCKING . . .

(*slight pause*)

And no one . . . NO ONE . . . can take it away from you.

(*a secret*)

At night, when you shut off the lights, I jerk off . . . It's great . . .

(*abrupt blackout*)

I have this fantasy . . . a recurring dream really . . . of going to bed with the very first woman I met who wasn't related to my mother or some other friend of the family. I just want to take her to bed and fuck the yelping shit out of her. In the dream, I'm a lot more romantic. I was fourteen when it started. During those days, I was the pride of the senior class . . . a freshman with a face beyond question. In other words, I could buy booze. Anyway, I met her, a nineteen year old freshman on my first ski weekend. I'd already had a pint of courage and—for the first time—conversation came easily. We danced and drank and talked and grew friendly as the night grew late. I remember holding her closely—during the few slow dances the band was merciful enough to play—and kissing her for the first time while they played, "Hey Jude". It wasn't planned. It just happened. After that, we didn't dance. I don't think we even heard the music. We just sat in our corner and kissed.

(*lights up. Jeremy is sitting on the balance beam miming his encounter with his dream woman.*)

I remember sensing other people around (*kisses*) but I didn't care. (*kisses*) And she didn't care. We just wanted to kiss. (*kisses*) Long . . . (*kisses*) passionate . . . (*kisses*) kisses. It was like a dirty movie.

(*a sense of excitement builds in Jeremy*)

Our tongues moved in time with the music.

(*kisses*)

Her hand caressed the back of my neck; my hand, daringly, massaged her thigh.

(*kisses*)

She nibbled on my neck—and then my chest. I let my hand slip under her sweater. She didn't protest. She muttered encouragements. "Yes . . . yes! Oh, yes! More! Don't stop!" I felt her bra and pushing under it, fondled her breasts. We drew closer to each other. It was perfect.

(*he breaks away*)

And then, reality ended. I was, after all, a catholic high school freshman with a curfew and a religious chaperon to enforce the rules. We were separated.

(*slight pause*)

But, in my dream, we left together.
(*he beckons and she joins him*)

The halls and doors of the hotel sped by. There were no robed guards, no friends, no roommates to keep us apart. In a flash, we were in her room. The door is locked and she is already in bed. Her skirt is pulled up around her waist; her legs are spread; she is calling me to her. And I kneel over her, touching her again; feeling her sweater against my hands; pushing the material upwards, out of the way; letting my fingers play with her breasts . . . her nipples . . . and she . . . she is quickly undressing me; unbuckling my belt and unzippering my pants; working my pants and my underwear down around my knees . . .

(the lights begin to fade)

She is holding me firmly; pulling me towards her; on top of her. When we kiss again, it is electric—the most exciting moment of my life. Her arms . . . her hands are all over me . . . commanding me . . . pressing me against her. I feel her legs rise around me. She moans and groans and wimpers. She begs me to take her. Take her. And I do . . . I do. Again. Again and again. Harder and harder. Faster . . . quicker . . . harder . . . deeper . . . I take . . .

(a spotlight clicks on suddenly and begins searching for Jeremy)

NO!! SHIT!! NO!!

(Jeremy can be seen darting back and forth, ducking down as low as he can—almost running on his haunches.)

LEAVE ME ALONE! DAMN YOU! THIS ISN'T FAIR! IT'S NOT FAIR!

(The light catches him sitting on his haunches, clutching his knees. His head is down. His back is turned away from the source of the light. He vaguely resembles an ape.)
(softly)

You shouldn't . . . shouldn't . . . shouldn't . . .

(*a grunt*)

What do you want?

(*a grunt*)

No.

(*a louder grunt*)

NO!!

(*The spotlight moves away from Jeremy and to the swing. It begins to move by itself. Grunts and gentle jungle sounds are heard.*)

NO!!

(*organ grinder music and passive ape sounds*)

Go to hell!

(*abrupt blackout*)

SCENE SEVEN

(*dawn in the jungle. The woman watches him with interest.*)

JEREMY

(*looking more haggard than before.*)

Hello . . .

I'm hungry . . .

Talk to me . . . please . . .

(*Jeremy begins to feel his way along the glass—trying to see out. He is desperate. She in turn, is pleased and follows his movements with great interest.*)

Are you still out there. I can't hear you. Talk to me. Please . . . I'm hungry . . .

You haven't fed me in . . . what . . . days. It's been days. I don't know how many. I can't tell. Don't leave me alone.

Please . . . I want to talk to you . . .

I want . . .

Don't . . .

Please . . .

Please . . .

Come back . . . I need you . . .

Don't leave me . . . Please . . .

Talk to me . . .

TALK TO ME . . .

(*blackout*)

SCENE EIGHT

(*darkness*)

(*Two spotlights pick up two circus posters. One is of a lady in a tiger suit holding a whip. The other is of a huge gorilla pounding his chest.*)

(*Circus music is heard.*)

(*A grunt.*)

(*Jeremy hears the sound and turns looking for it—not sure that he has actully heard it. He replies with a weak grunt of his own.*)

(*A louder, stronger grunt.*)

(*Jeremy seems relieved by the sound. He replies again with a louder grunt. He seems to look for the source of the sound.*)

(*Still louder and stronger grunts.*)

(*Jeremy answers in kind.*)

(*Grunts and screams.*)

(*Jeremy grunts and screams and, looking at the poster, finally gets the idea. He turns in the direction of the sound and grunts and screams again—this time, pounding his chest. The moves are awkward and tentative.*)

(*A grunt—sounding more positive, less commanding.*)

(*Jeremy is pleased. He repeats the routine.*)

(*The lights focus on the swing which again begins to move.*)

(*Jeremy sits on the swing as a child in a park might.*)

(*Angry grunts and screams.*)

(*Jeremy seems startled and uncertain. He looks at the poster and sees the picture of the ape. He slowly rises, uncertain, and stands on the swing. He grunts, asking for approval.*)

(*A reply: an approving grunt.*)

(*Jeremy is overjoyed. He begins to grunt and scream, swinging from side to side.*)

(*The door in the rear opens. Jeremy runs to it, half as a man, half as an ape. There is a banana inside. He takes it, grunting his thanks. He squats down and eats.*)

(*The door closes. The lights fade.*)

SCENE NINE

(The same as before. In contrast, however, Jeremy's actions are no longer tentative. He is a confident ape-man. He uses the entire space (the swing, the beam, etc.) as might a particularly active gorilla. At this point, the metamorphosis is complete. It should take the form of a gorilla dance ending with the ape's demand for a banana. At that point, the door will open and he will be fed.)

(Jeremy eats as the lights dim.)

SCENE TEN

(*Gloria, dressed like the figure in the poster, is in the cage with the ape. She commands him to do a variety of tricks and rewards him periodically with pieces of fruit. It is, by and large, a circus act. And yet, there is something more in the way she treats him. There is something erotic in her handling of the ape. For his part, he responds as would a pet.*)

(*After the act is completed, she sits him on the balance beam and gives him something to eat.*)

GLORIA

Yes, I do think you were a wise choice. I am pleased. You've done better . . . responded quicker than I expected. You should be happy. You learn very well.
(*slight pause*)
Do you need anything?
(*a grunt*)
Good, I'm glad. I'll bring you something special later. You'll like that.
(*a grunt*)
Now, *stay*. Stay well.
(*to herself*)
Yes, you were a good choice. The first one should be easy. This experiment was a success.

(*blackout*)

SCENE ELEVEN

(*In much the same manner of scene eight, the ape does his dance. He is energetic . . . and happy. When he is finished, he goes to the door and awaits his reward. The door does not open. No banana. The ape becomes frantic. He does his dance again—only the dance, this time, is even more energetic. He is trying harder, working for all he is worth. His grunts and screams are louder and, perhaps, a little desperate.*)

(*He goes to the door again, banging it to demand the expected banana. Once again, the door does not open. No banana.*)

(*The gorilla screams and pounds his chest in rage.*)

(*blackout*)

EPILOGUE

(*A final tableaux: the gorilla sits on the floor (near the door) resting heavily against the wall. He is a pathetic figure. It is possible that he no longer has the strength—or the will—to swat the fly that eventually lands on him.*)

(*He lets out a single, sorrowful grunt as the play ends.*)

Two: ICE AGE

ICE AGE
a play in eight scenes

In memory of Anthony Palazzo

"I lie the truth"
—from the film, THE 4TH MAN

Cast:

The Storyteller:	A man in his 70's.
The Innkeeper:	A woman in her late 50's.
The Clerk:	A woman in her 30's.
The Handyman:	A rustic, outdoors man of 30.
The Chambermaid:	A woman in her 20's.
The Guest:	A man in his 20's.

Place:
A secluded, somewhat threadbare, New England Inn.

Time:

Winter

PROLOGUE

(*An old man, the Storyteller, sits on the sofa. He leans heavily on his cane, speaking to the moment's only available audience, the Chambermaid. Throughout his discourse, she busies herself with her chores, acknowledging his presence but never really paying attention.*)

STORYTELLER

Soup in a can ain't real. I ain't gonna argue with you . . . I know what's served around here ain't real. I don't need to read the labels—all that bullshit about NATURAL IN-GREDIENTS—that's a crock of shit. Food from a can tastes like food from a can. Period! When I had the chance —before I moved here—I did all my own cooking—made all my own soups—everything from scratch. Think you could do that? (*shakes head*) I doubt it. You wouldn't know what to do first. That's the truth. The world's forgotten how. Everything's gotten easy. Boiled down and simplified . . . put in cans, wrapped in plastic, bottled in cardboard with the straw built right in! They've robbed you of your money and your brains. I know its true because if you had brains, you wouldn't waste your money on things you don't need. I never owned a can opener. Everything was fresh. Real NATURAL FOOD! When you start with a tomato—a real, fresh, sweet-smelling tomato—when you hold it in your hand— you don't need a can opener. Kids today can't go to the bathroom without tools. Hell, they can't even get laid without special equipment. Crazy world . . . Damn crazy . . .

(*gunshot is heard [off]. The Storyteller stops for a moment cocking his head in the direction of the sound. Similarly, the Chambermaid stops. A look of dismay crosses her face. She appears as a woman concerned with only one thing: she will ultimately have to clean up the mess. It should be obvious—somewhat—that the gunshot is not an altogether unfamiliar sound. The Storyteller and the Chambermaid continue . . .)*

STORYTELLER

Damn crazy world! If people . . . if you people . . . just went back to doing for yourselves without depending on some quick fix, silver platter remedy things would be a damn sight better. I remember how it was. If you'd listen, I could tell you. If . . .

VOICE

[*off*] JUDITH!

STORYTELLER

(*Derisive*) The sheets need cleaning.

(*blackout*)

SCENE ONE

(*Enter the Innkeeper, followed by a new Guest. The Desk Clerk, the Chambermaid, the Handyman and the Storyteller are all present. The Handyman exits past the Guest.*)

INNKEEPER

I run a good, clean, respectable house. This is my home. I let people come here—I let them come and live with me . . . under my roof. I don't allow no cursing, yelling or fighting. That's a rule. This is a happy, a pleasant house. Remember that. Don't butt into anyone's business. I won't permit it. That's another rule. If you can remember them you can stay. If not, don't bother signing in. You won't last.

GUEST

I understand.

INNKEEPER

This is a small Inn in a small town . . .

GUEST

I know . . .

INNKEEPER

(*Ignoring*) Everyone in this room (*They are observing the proceedings*) . . . I know. I've known most of them—they've lived with me or near me—for a very long time. I'll take care of them long before I even think of you.

GUEST

I need a room.

INNKEEPER

It's your decision.

GUEST

I'd like to stay.

INNKEEPER

As you wish. (*Pointing*) Fill out a card and give it to the girl. I require two weeks in advance. I don't give anything back if it don't work out . . . if you leave early. Rent is due every Monday. Dinner is at six; breakfast at seven. I don't serve luncheons—there's plenty of food to last through the day if you sit with us. If not (*Shrugs*) . . . you're on your own. The kitchen stays closed most of the time.

GUEST

I'm sure everything will work out.

INNKEEPER

I'll insist on it. (*A brief pause*) Someone will show you to your room when you're ready. (*Begins to exit*)

GUEST

Thank you.

(*The Innkeeper stops, looks back, but doesn't respond. It is an awkward moment. It is as if she simply has nothing left to say. The Innkeeper finally reaches back into her repertoire, speaks one line and exits.*)

INNKEEPER

It's almost six. DINNER is at six.

(*He moves to the desk. The Storyteller rises to join him.*)

GUEST

(*Cordial*) Hi!

CLERK

Hello.

GUEST

I'd like to register.

(The Clerk puts a card and pen in front of the Guest. The Storyteller interrupts.)

STORYTELLER

You handled her just right.

GUEST

Excuse me?

STORYTELLER

You let her talk . . . you didn't interrupt . . . you listened. That's important. You've made a good start here. You should last as long time. Yes, I suspect a fair piece of time. I think you'll enjoy our little house. Speak with me later— after you unpack, after dinner—and I'll give you a few tips, let you in on a few secrets about our *host*. I've been here long enough to be useful. (*A brief pause*) Goodbye for now. (*exits*)

CLERK

He just likes to talk. I hope you won't be bored. I mean, you're new here; you haven't heard his stories.

GUEST

I'm sure we'll get along. There won't be a problem.

CLERK

I hope not. Try to be polite—listen to his stories. Or pretend. (*Sheepishly*) I'm afraid we all do that.

GUEST

I understand. You don't want to hurt him . . .

CLERK

You're kind. (*Smiles*) I think the old man's right. You should be here for awhile. I hope so, anyway.

GUEST

So do I. I need a place to live . . . some place to rest for a little while. I don't wanna move too quickly.

CLERK

I think you'll like it here. My mother is usually a pretty good judge . . . she owns this house.

GUEST

She's your . . .

CLERK

Don't let her frighten you. She's a little rough at first—but that's the business talking. She's not like that.

GUEST

I'm glad to hear it.

CLERK

You'll see, she'll change.

GUEST

Maybe we could meet later. You could fill me in on what I should know and . . .

CLERK

The Storyteller—that's what we call him—he'll tell you everything.

GUEST

I'd like to get to know *all* my neighbors.

CLERK

That's nice.

GUEST

We could meet for a drink—after dinner.

CLERK

I don't drink.

GUEST

Coffee?

CLERK

The old man will keep you busy. Besides, I have to work . . .

GUEST

Tomorrow?

CHAMBERMAID

(*Interrupting*) Are you ready to see your room, sir?

CLERK

(*Holding up key*) I hope you enjoy your stay.

GUEST

I'm sure I will.

CLERK

Goodbye . . . for now.

CHAMBERMAID

This way, sir.

GUEST

Yes . . . thank you.

(*They exit. The Clerk follows them with her eyes. The Inn-keeper enters from beneath the stairway. She hugs Clerk from behind.*)

CLERK

(*Still looking*) I like this one.

INNKEEPER

I know.

CLERK

I hope he stays.

INNKEEPER

He will.

CLERK

Thank you.

(The Innkeeper kisses the Clerk gently on the cheek. The Storyteller enters leaning heavily on his cane. He stops, looks around, addresses the Innkeeper.)

STORYTELLER

(Looking up) Is he . . .

INNKEEPER

A moment ago.

(The Storyteller nods. Walks a few hobbling steps. Stops. He stretches grandly, cracking his back. During the course of this activity, he "loses" the cane, hanging it on the back of a chair. The Storyteller crosses the room with a brisk, spry step, dropping into his chair with amazing ease and grace. The Chambermaid enters with a tray of drinks. As she offers the Storyteller a glass, the two woman move towards the Chambermaid. Ultimately, everyone has a drink.)

STORYTELLER

(Savoring drink) I allow myself two drinks . . . The first to warm and awaken an aging brain and then again, at this hour, at moments like this . . .

INNKEEPER

At moments of celebration . . .

STORYTELLER

At moments like this . . . to lull a cranky old machine back towards rest. Towards the close of day—and the night. It is a wonderful, a most civilized custom, prescribed by my most considerate caretaker. *(Salute)* My doctor doesn't give a damn if I get dizzy or fall down . . . if I spend my days trapped within the folds of my bedcovers and my nights asleep in my chair, before the fire. Hell, he probably sees himself as some sort of domestic missionary, bent on saving each of you from hours of boring, unproductive intercourse. *(Looks around)* Whatever the reason, I salute the bastard. I get the advice I pay for; we both feel great.

CLERK

(*Meek*) I hope he stays.

STORYTELLER

The young man will stay. He was a good choice.

CHAMBERMAID

I hope so. I'm growing a little tired of strangers. (*To Clerk*) Luck hasn't been with any of us lately. (*To Innkeeper*) This one doesn't look any different than your last . . . choice . . .

CLERK

I liked him . . .

CHAMBERMAID

He didn't last.

INNKEEPER

I do the best . . .

CHAMBERMAID

He left at an inappropriate moment. We needed him.

CLERK

I don't remember his name.

CHAMBERMAID

We deserve better.

INNKEEPER

I do the best that I can. I have to chose—to make the decision—on my own. You don't help. Sometimes I think you hide whenever someone new comes. I have to holler just to find you . . . sometimes. That's how you want it. You leave it to me—all of you. My choice! YOUR CHOICE! I have to be here, ready, waiting—and all alone—when they come down that damn road. (*Brief pause*) There aren't many. I do my best.

CHAMBERMAID

I have work to do! I have *my* own job . . .

STORYTELLER

Our young man will stay. (*To Innkeeper*) He was a *good* choice.

INNKEEPER

Thank you.

STORYTELLER

(*To Chambermaid*) A very good . . . a sound choice.

CLERK

I'm glad (*Pause*) I'd like to talk to him . . . tomorrow.

INNKEEPER

I'll take him a newspaper . . . in the morning.

CHAMBERMAID

(*sarcastic*) And I'll bring him fresh linens every day.

STORYTELLER

He shouldn't ask for anything. That's important. Let him depend on us. *LET HIM DEPEND ON US*. That's the key.

INNKEEPER

I know . . .

STORYTELLER

And no fighting. I won't stand for it. I won't have a silly bitch—young or old—ruining *our* vacation. Do you understand me?

(*The Innkeeper and Chambermaid are silent—obviously stung.*)

CLERK

Yes.

STORYTELLER

I think I'll have another drink—an extra, *my third*—to celebrate. I expect good times. Here! (*To Chambermaid*)

You know what I drink. (*Thrusts glass at her*) Make it strong. Let me taste it this time.

(*The Chambermaid takes the glass. She is angry enough to pause; to consider a reply. Ultimately, she exits quickly—and silently*)

STORYTELLER

Do you think she's mad with me? (*Quickly, not waiting for an answer*) Too bad! She shouldn't have raised her voice; she can say anything she likes—don't get me wrong—but, dammit, I will not deal with her anger or her attitude. I don't need that right now. It's not right. (*Slight pause*) We may want to replace her. Yes, we may . . .

INNKEEPER

I'll talk to her.

STORYTELLER

I feel younger. Can you believe that? 73 years old and suddenly I feel younger. Not young, but getting better. She really put enough in my drink the first time. I was just trying to annoy her. I think I'll have an extra drink every night. That really will annoy her. All that extra work. Christ, I can hear the complaints now . . . banging the bottles, throwing the ice at the glass, missing, cursing . . . God, I wish I could hear it all. (*To Innkeeper*) I used to drink quite alot. Do you think I should have an extra drink?

INNKEEPER

You can have anything you want.

STORYTELLER

You don't care about me. I'll call my doctor. (*Slight pause*) There shouldn't be a problem.

(*Slow fade out as the scene ends.*)

SCENE TWO

(Guest bedroom. Everything else is in darkness. The Clerk is at the door with a tray of coffee.)

CLERK

I brought an extra cup.

GUEST

Excuse me?

CLERK

With your coffee. You said you wanted to have a drink. I brought an extra cup. I hope you don't mind.

GUEST

No. Not at all. That's fine.

CLERK

I can always come back.

GUEST

That's alright.

CLERK

I just thought you'd like some coffee. After unpacking and all.

GUEST

That was nice of you.

CLERK

I know how hard travelling can be. I mean, I can imagine. I haven't been anywhere myself. The house takes up all our time . . . but I see a lot standing at that desk. Everyone looks so tired after they check in.

GUEST

You're right about me. I am very tired.

CLERK

Do you want me to leave?

GUEST

No! Not at all. I'd really enjoy the company. I've been on the road for quite awhile. Most of the time I'm alone. I'd really enjoy the company.

CLERK

I'm glad. (*Awkward pause*) So, how about some coffee?

GUEST

Great.

CLERK

How do you like it?

GUEST

Just milk.

CLERK

I'll have it ready for you in a minute.

GUEST

How long have you worked here?

CLERK

I've lived here all my life. I was born here.

(*The lights fade somewhat. The Clerk and the Guest remain visible, but inaudible as they go through their tea party routine. The lights fade up in the living room. The Innkeeper is present. She is drinking. In fact, she is drunk. She speaks to herself and the Storyteller, who simply sits, leaning forward and listening.*)

INNKEEPER

This *was* my home. Sometime ago I built it . . . with help— I will admit that—but it was my idea. And my home. I bought the land at a time when wilderness was cheap . . . before city folks from New York came to civilize the waste-land . . . and worked to make it mine. We cleared the trees and the brush and the rocks . . . there were rocks every-where . . . just under the surface . . . casually hidden. That was the hard part. There wasn't a place we could go, an inch of earth we could dig through, that wasn't blocked by a rock . . . something that was either too sharp or too heavy to handle. But, *WE MANAGED*. We cleared the land, moved rocks, boulders, roots, stumps, pushed back every-thing you see surrounding us and built our house. It was hard . . . maybe we could have found an easier way, maybe we could have hired someone, but we didn't. We built this house *by ourselves*. We built it with our strength and imag-ination. That's what we gave this place—strength and imagination. It was a good time. It should have lasted. Nothing has been the same since. (*Pause*) I've been ram-bling. Forgive me. It's just a mood . . . something I'm going through at the moment. Who knows? Maybe I'm getting old . . . changing . . . becoming more like . . . like you. (*A brief pause*) I know why you like him. He listens. He lets you chatter on. He doesn't interrupt. And, he doesn't scare easily. That's important, you know. I scare off half the young men who come here. They never get past first im-pressions. (*To Storyteller with zest*) BOO! (*Laughs*) That's me: the wild wierd wood-witch; the black widow out to snare young, unsuspecting men. (*Softer*) Draw them in, tie them up, drain them . . . dry. Rob them of spirit . . . of soul . . . and whatever cash they happen to have left . . . here's your check, get out . . . just another listless corpse thrown back into . . . what? . . . (*Shrugs*). No one would notice. That's the reality of this place. No one ever does. (*Softer*) Boo . . . I never wanted to be the scary one. It's not fair. (*Pause. The Storyteller rises, turns and leaves. The Inn-keeper is left alone—unanswered.*) IT'S NOT FAIR.

(*The lights fade out on the Innkeeper and back up on the Guest and the Clerk. They are now more comfortable with each other.*)

CLERK

We don't get new people here very often. You were an unexpected, pleasant surprise. I mean, you're different. I
know everyone else. I told you, I was born here. Most of
them have been here, with me, all my life. I know everything about them—everything interesting and all the
boring stuff, too. Most of it is boring anyway. Nothing
happens

GUEST

That can't be true.

CLERK

But it is! There are no secrets left. This is a small commu-
nity. I mean, everything is left open for everyone to see. We
don't have any secrets left. (*Slight pause*) Everyone will be
very interested in you.

GUEST

I'm nothing special.

CLERK

But you are! I hope they won't bother you too much.

GUEST

Don't worry about it. Everything will be fine. I promised
your mother, remember. Besides, I can use the company.
I've been alone quite a bit lately. It'll be a nice change.

CLERK

The old man was right. You were a good choice.

GUEST

What do you mean?

CLERK

That's what he says whenever Mother lets someone stay
here. You were her "choice". Which isn't true . . . I know
that . . . but he sees it that way. To tell you the truth, most
people who come by don't even stay. My Mother scares
them, I guess. I hope you'll stay . . . for awhile.

GUEST

I told your Mother, I need a place. I think this is it. I want to stay put for awhile. It would be a nice change. I mean, hell, I've been moving about quite a bit lately. It's time to stop . . . for now.

CLERK

I'm glad. I'd like to get to know you.

GUEST

I'd like that, too. How about some more coffee?

CLERK

I'll have the maid bring you a fresh pot.

GUEST

Can't you stay?

CLERK

It's getting late. I have to lock up.

GUEST

Can you come back?

CLERK

Mother wouldn't approve.

GUEST

Just for a little while.

CLERK

You should get some sleep.

GUEST

I'm not tired.

CLERK

You're overtired—from your trip, remember. Once you lie down . . . (*Shrugs*). We can talk tomorrow.

(*Slow fade as she exits.*)

SCENE THREE

(*Darkness. The sound of crickets is heard. Lights fade up dimly on the living room. The Innkeeper and the Storyteller are seated opposite each other. He is reading a newspaper. She is knitting.*)
(*Pause. A piercing scream is heard. The Storyteller and the Innkeeper look at each other for a moment.*)

INNKEEPER

He screamed.

STORYTELLER

Yes. I think I will have another drink.

(*Slow fade as they return to their activities. The lights fade up on the bedroom area. The Guest is seated on the bed, sitting up, a look of terror on his face.*)
(*NOTE: It should be obvious throughout what follows that we are watching a dream.*)
(*A pair of black hands take hold of the Guest and draw him backwards onto the mattress. The Clerk appears, almost out of nowhere, and stands before him. She speaks in clipped, mechanical phrases.*)

CLERK

I brought an extra cup . . .
(*She begins to undress*)
You wanted something to drink . . .
Thought you'd like coffee . . .
How about some coffee . . .
Coffee . . .
With milk . . .
You look tired . . .
You should rest . . .
Relax . . .

You were an unexpected surprise . . .
There are no secrets left . . .
Everything open . . .
Everything . . .
Everyone . . .
Interested in you . . .
Very interested . . .
I'd like to get to know you . . .
You were a good choice . . .
(*The Clerk, dressed in a bra and panties, climbs into bed
with the Guest.*)

You were a very good choice. I hope you stay.
(*She climbs on top of him, and begins kissing him passionately. He does not respond—this is a nightmare, afterall.
She rubs against him, kissing first his lips, then his neck
and, then again, his chest. The Guest stares at her with an
incredulous, almost comic look of horror. The Handyman
appears.*)

HANDYMAN

You gotta tell me what's so fuckin' special about you. I
mean, hell, you've got this whole place acting like you're
some kinda gift from God. The old man is carrying on like
we never had Guests in this dump before. The Old Lady is
knitting you a sweater. Do you believe it? That Old Harpy!
Shit! They've all gone crazy . . . over you. It doesn't make
sense. The bosses' daughter—that cute piece of trash
you've got there—is acting like you're the last customer
through the door with a fuckin' cock; a real big, real important shit! That's a lie, one of the great lies, if you ask me. I
don't see a God, a Saint, a Savior or anything special. All I
see is a wimp . . . a wimp who walked in on a bunch of
desperate people and lucked out. You've found a great,
warm comfortable bed to hide in. Enjoy it. But, don't get too
comfortable. There is a snake in that bed. It's gonna bite
you. It won't take long. Soon. I'm gonna be there—just like
now—and then, friend, I'll fix you. I'll finish the job. (*He

sits on the bed next to the Guests head. He grabs his face and turns him toward him.) Remember what I said.

(*Long pause. Lights fade very slowly. Total darkness.*)

GUEST
(*Screaming*) *NOOO!*

(*Lights up abruptly. The nightmare is over; the Guest is awake, shaken and more than a little afraid. He is alone in his room. The Storyteller and the Innkeeper are seated as before.*)
Christ!

STORYTELLER
He's up.

INNKEEPER
I thought I heard something. (*Rings bell*) Should I mention that screaming?

STORYTELLER
Not this time. Let's see what happens.

INNKEEPER
You think he'll bring it up?

STORYTELLER
Let's see what happens.

INNKEEPER
I just thought ... he'll expect me to say something. I warned him to be quiet.

STORYTELLER
Shut up! It's not necessary—right now. (*Chambermaid enters*) Let me handle him. I know what to do. He won't ...

CHAMBERMAID
(*Contemptuous*) You rang?

STORYTELLER

She did.

INNKEEPER

He's up. Make sure everyone knows.

CHAMBERMAID

Everyone knows. It's no secret. We all heard him.

STORYTELLER

Just do what you're told!

CHAMBERMAID

HEY!

STORYTELLER

Do your job! Go up there and make his bed. See if he needs anything. Then, come back and tell us what he says. EVERYTHING HE SAYS.

CHAMBERMAID

Anything else?

STORYTELLER

Don't you ever interrupt me again. Understand?

(Pause)

CHAMBERMAID

(Very low) You crazy old man . . . what's wrong with you? You getting a little soft . . . Do you think it's all real? Is that it? You're a fraud. That's reality. This rundown rest home is a fraud. A lie. It's all a lie.

STORYTELLER

Get to work!

CHAMBERMAID

I know my job. My role . . . *(She exits)*

STORYTELLER

Get rid of her!

INNKEEPER

I'll talk to her.

STORYTELLER

(*Shouting*) *GET RID OF HER!*

(*Throughout the proceeding, the Guest has been dressing. He now enters.*)

GUEST

Excuse me.

STORYTELLER

Oh! Forgive me. I shouldn't be yelling like that. It's very rude. Not to mention "bad for me". My doctor would have a fit. He doesn't like it when I get excited. It was silly of me. A little domestic problem I let get the better of me. (*To Innkeeper*) I'm sorry.

INNKEEPER

It wasn't your fault. She was rude. I *will* speak to her.

STORYTELLER

(*To Guest*) I hope my behavior didn't disturb you.

GUEST

Not at all.

INNKEEPER

How was your first night?

GUEST

Not bad. I was comfortable enough . . . I guess. It's a nice room.

STORYTELLER

But . . .

GUEST

I don't know. I just woke up from the most incredible nightmare. It was weird. I was in my room and . . . (*looks at Innkeeper*) Well, I can't remember most of it. It scared me. I can tell you that.

INNKEEPER

That explains a lot.

GUEST

I don't understand.

STORYTELLER

You screamed.

GUEST

Oh, God!

INNKEEPER

You had us concerned.

GUEST

I'm sorry.

STORYTELLER

It's alright. We all have lapses. I'm just glad there was nothing wrong; just a bad dream.

GUEST

I can't imagine . . . I don't understand what caused it.

STORYTELLER

You should be more careful about what you eat. I'll bet that's it. You won't find too many nightmares up here. We eat simple foods. Simple foods don't stir the system all up. You should remember that. Take a look at the people around you. I mean, this part of the country. We're a very calm people. Nothing exciting in our days or our stomachs. You stick around, you'll see what I mean. You'll learn . . .

GUEST

I thought I'd take a walk into town. Is there anything interesting I should look for?

STORYTELLER

Even small towns *like this one* can be interesting.

GUEST

That's not what I meant.

STORYTELLER

I know. Ask the girl at the desk. She'll give you a map.

GUEST

Thanks.

(*He crosses to desk. The Clerk enters just as he gets there. The Storyteller and the Innkeeper watch for a moment, look at each other knowingly, then go back to their respective paper and knitting.*)

CLERK

Oh! Hello.

GUEST

Good morning.

CLERK

Did you sleep well?

GUEST

(*A little uncomfortable*) Eh, well, I guess so. I was a little restless, I guess.

CLERK

That's nothing to worry about. It was your first night— after a hard day travelling. Your system was upset. That would explain it.

GUEST

You're probably right. I guess.

CLERK

Just forget it. And relax. What can I get you?

GUEST

A map . . . of town.

CLERK

That's easy. Here. Enjoy yourself—but don't overdo it. I want you to enjoy this place too. A good night's sleep is important.

GUEST

Thanks. (*He starts to exit*)

CLERK

I'll bring you some more coffee. Tonight.

(*The Guest looks back. The idea disturbs him somewhat.*)

GUEST

Eh, . . . yeah . . . sure . . .

(*He begins to exit but runs into the Handyman just inside the doorway.*)

HANDYMAN

Well, Hello! You must be the new one everyone is talking about. Welcome. I hope you enjoy your stay. If you need anything—anything that needs fixing—that's what I do— just let me know.

(*The Guest is visibly shaken. He is face-to-face with an image from his dream; an image he doesn't remember seeing earlier.*)

GUEST

Sure.

HANDYMAN

I'll have that window fixed before you get back.

GUEST

What . . .

HANDYMAN

Your window rattles. I'll fix it—so it don't disturb you. It'll be done before you know it.

GUEST

Okay . . . thanks.

HANDYMAN

I'll talk to you later.

(*The Handyman crosses to the desk. The Guest takes a quick look after the Handyman, then exits. The Handyman, Clerk, Storyteller and Innkeeper look at each other. They seem pleased.*)

(*Slow fade to black.*)

SCENE FOUR

(The Guest and The Storyteller are sitting in the living room. It is fairly dark. During the course of the scene, the Chambermaid will enter the Guest's room and turn down the bed. While she is there, the Clerk will enter with the coffee. She will sit and wait for the Chambermaid to leave. There is obvious animosity between the two.)

STORYTELLER

There was this man, a Sheriff as I remember, who built his house by a lake. I want you to understand, before I start, that this was a good man, a good Christian man, who lived a good, sound life. *(The Guest nods, acknowledging)* This Sheriff was sitting—alone—on his porch one evening. Sun was down, but there was still a little light—a dark sort of grey. But anyway, he's looking out over his piece of land and lake when he sees something floating—a black shape floating on his piece of lake just off his dock. The problem is, it's too dark to make out just what this is . . . floating on the water. He's curious, you see. It's out there . . . he doesn' know what . . . on his water . . . and he's curious. He tells himself—as the Sheriff, I guess—that he should investigate—and he does. He takes his light and goes out on the dock and looks out at the black shape. He sees what it is. *(The Storyteller takes a slow sip and a deliberately long pause)* I've told this story before. No one ever believes this part. The Sheriff shined his flashlight down onto the water and into the black eyes of a huge catfish. These eyes were as large as giant, black plums—which gives you and idea of how monsterous this fish really was. The Sheriff and this great fish stared at each other for a long second before the bigger of the two said goodbye with a great splash. He was gone. The Sheriff never saw him again. (*Pause*) The problem—for the Sheriff—was that he saw the fish. It was there. *It was real!* His mistake was telling other people what he saw. They wrote about it in the town paper, made a big thing about it. They laughed about it in the bars and behind his back. In the end, they laughed at him. He wasn't Sheriff anymore. He was just a man who saw a fish with eyes the size of plums. Last I heard, he died on that dock. They found him with a camera on his lap.

                              GUEST
What's the point?

                           STORYTELLER
There isn't one. It happened. Period.

                              GUEST
A little folklore?

                           STORYTELLER
Nope. It didn't happen around here. Things like that just don't happen in these parts. I told you—we live a very simple life. God saved the surprises for more distant places.

                              GUEST
That's too bad.

                           STORYTELLER
Not really. It depends on your point of view, I guess. We see things differently up here. I kinda like it the way it is. We're in charge of what happens. The Sheriff wasn't. Maybe that's the point.

(*The Clerk is walking slowly around the bed, running her fingers lightly across the sheet. She sits on the bed and then lies back as ...*)

(*Lights fade to black.*)

SCENE FIVE

(The Innkeeper is alone. She appears very happy. The Guest enters.)

INNKEEPER

Oh, good! Come in. Sit down and talk to me. *(The Guest is taken by surprise. This is, after all, out of character for the Innkeeper.)*

GUEST

I was just going to my room. I wanted to write . . .

INNKEEPER

Oh, that can wait. Come on . . . I can use the company . . . and the conversation.

GUEST

Just for a little while, . . okay?

INNKEEPER

That's all I ask. *(The Guest sits)* Do you like it here?

GUEST

Yeah, sure.

INNKEEPER

I realize you haven't been here very long—just a few days really—but you seem to be fitting in nicely. Everyone has good things to say about you.

GUEST

I'm glad.

INNKEEPER

I never asked—what do you do?

GUEST

I freelance mostly. I travel around, paint—mostly for mag-azines—and pick up whatever work I can. I've gotten to see quite a lot of the country; met a lot of interesting people along the way. It's a good way to live . . . at least for me.

INNKEEPER

And now you're ready to settle down.

GUEST

For awhile. I needed a change of pace.

INKEEPER

Would you consider staying on—here? I could find some-thing for you.

GUEST

I don't understand.

INNKEEPER

I've been thinking of making some changes around the place. There'd be a job for you if you're interested.

GUEST

I'm . . .

INNKEEPER

I couldn't pay much . . . you can see there isn't much around here . . . but you'd have your room and all the food you could want plus a small salary and enough free time to paint or do whatever.

GUEST

I'm not really looking for a job.

INNKEEPER

That's okay. It was just an idea. Something for you to con-sider. Your room is yours for as long as you want it.

GUEST

Thank you. I'd like to stay for a little while.

INNKEEPER

Don't you like it here?

GUEST

Very much. I just need to move around . . . that's how I am. A wanderlust. I'm never satisifed with one place for long.

INNKEEPER

I thought you wanted to change.

GUEST

Not really. I wanted to rest, that's all. (*Long pause. The Innkeeper looks upset*) What's wrong?

INNKEEPER

My daughter won't go with you.

GUEST

What do you mean?

INNKEEPER

I will not permit it. It is out of the question—absolutely out of the question. She was born in this house. *NOT IN A HOSPITAL—THIS HOUSE!* I will not have her trapsing around the country. This is her home. This is where she will stay. I will not discuss anything else. Do you understand me?

GUEST

Yes . . .

INNKEEPER

You'll just have to stay here with her . . . that's all. It's time to settle down. You can travel like everyone else—once a year for a few days—if you really have to, but that's it. This is where the two of you live. It's your home.

GUEST

I don't know what the fuck you're talking about!

INNKEEPER

(*Braying*) Don't you dare use that "language" with me. I will not tolerate it.

GUEST

I have no intention of living here with or without your daughter. When I leave, I leave alone. If she leaves—that's her choice. She won't be with me no matter what. Do *YOU* understand?

INNKEEPER

NO.

GUEST

I'm leaving.

INNKEEPER

No you're not. I haven't finished with you yet. I have more to say. This is my place. I make the rules.

GUEST

FUCK YOU. (*Moves to door*) I'm leaving now. I'll be back for my bag later.

INNKEEPER

(*Quiet*) Good luck.

(*The Handyman is in the doorway.*)

HANDYMAN

Oh, hello again.

GUEST

Hi . . .

HANDYMAN

I did a great job on that window. Right? I bet it's real quiet now.

GUEST

I can't hear it at all. Thank you.

HANDYMAN

Just want to keep you happy.

GUEST

Everyone seems concerned with my "happiness".

HANDYMAN

We like you.

GUEST

You don't even know me.

INNKEEPER

That's the point.

GUEST

I'm sorry. I don't know what it is . . . I'm just not comfortable . . .

HANDYMAN

Why not?

GUEST

I don't know. (*Slight pause*) Do you know of another Inn in this area?

HANDYMAN

You're leaving!

INNKEEPER

He hasn't paid his bill.

GUEST

I gave you two weeks in advance. (*Innkeeper simply shrugs*)

HANDYMAN

That's not very nice.

GUEST

I don't owe her a dime. Not one fuckin' dime!

HANDYMAN

There's a lady present—watch your mouth!

GUEST

Shit! Look, I just want to leave . . .

HANDYMAN

Pay your bill.

GUEST

I don't owe anything.

HANDYMAN

You can't leave without paying.

GUEST

Get out of my way.

INNKEEPER

He's not listening to reason. Maybe I should call the Sheriff.

HANDYMAN

I'll hold him 'til he gets here.

GUEST

This is crazy.

INNKEEPER

It's your choice. Just like when you checked in. I gave you a room. I fed you. I looked the other way when you went to bed with my daughter . . .

GUEST

WHAT!

INNKEEPER

UNDER MY ROOF. I heard the noise, but I looked the other way. She's old enough to make her own choices. I didn't say a word. But, I will not have you leave and take her or — worse — leave her. You will stay.

GUEST

I never touched your daughter.

INNKEEPER

Go to your room!

GUEST

I'm leaving.

HANDYMAN

If he tries to leave, I'll fix him. Call the Sheriff.

INNKEEPER

(*To Guest*) I know everyone in this town. I told you that once. If I tell the Sheriff what you did, he'll charge you with more than slipping out on the bill.

HANDYMAN

I'll fix you for that.

INNKEEPER

Go to your room . . . and think about it.

GUEST

You're crazy.

INNKEEPER

Maybe. Go to your room.

(*He starts to move in that direction. The Clerk enters from behind the counter*)

CLERK

I'll bring you coffee . . . later.

GUEST

It never happened.

INNKEEPER

I know what happens and what doesn't happen in this house. I know what is true and what is a lie. It's my choice.

GUEST

(*Retreating*) This is insane!

(*He exits into the bedroom. The Innkeeper crosses to the Clerk, kisses her and exits. The Handyman moves a chair by the door and sits. In the bedroom, the Guest furiously grabs his clothes and begins to pack. The Chambermaid enters. She takes a shirt from his hand and puts it in on the bed. She shakes her head ("No") and walks right up to him, taking him in her arms. He is totally overwhelmed by the insanity of the situation. The lights fade in the bedroom as she kisses him . . .*)

(*The Storyteller enters. He sees the Handyman seated by the door. The Handyman indicates upstairs. The Storyteller nods. He moves towards the Clerk who crosses to meet him. He kisses her gently, perhaps strokes her hair and leads her to the sofa. They both sit.*)

STORYTELLER

I've seen so many strange things—I can believe almost anything. The important thing is to remember those things that you *have* seen. No, that's not true. Remember the things you haven't seen. Most people can't do that. Most people don't understand the logic . . . (*Slight pause*) You're looking very pretty.

CLERK

Thank you.

STORYTELLER

I believe in Monsters. Did you know that? I've seen them more than once. (*She smiles*) Have I told you this before? You have a lovely smile. (*She smiles broadly*) Thank you.

(*Fade out.*)

SCENE SIX

(The Guest is in his room. Everyone else is in the living room. The Chambermaid addresses them.)

CHAMBERMAID

It's time you listen to me! *ALL OF YOU!* I am what keeps this operation living. Me! What I do! You jump in, take a bite and retreat. You leave him to me. I am the one that *heals* the wounds, stops the bleeding, distracts, soothes, cajoles, strokes and caresses the patient. *I AM THE ONE.* I've been to bed with him. Did you know that? He was ready to leave. He was packed and ready to leave. I soothed and stroked and sucked and sang that man to sleep. I unpacked his bag. I hung his clothes up, put his toothbrush and razor back in the bathroom, put his shoes under the bed and left that man pacified. I am the only reason he stays. I am *his* alternative, his way of brushing back your invasions. He doesn't look to that road anymore—he looks here! *TO ME!* And I go upstairs and change the sheets. *(Brief pause)* That's my life—my contribution to this machine. It is not enough. *YOU'VE GOT TO LISTEN TO ME!*

STORYTELLER

I don't have to do a thing. Not a fuckin' thing. *(To Innkeeper)* Rent her room.

CHAMBERMAID

You can't kick me out. I've been here too long.

STORYTELLER

Your room is vacant as of now. *(To Clerk)* Move her stuff—everything—into the basement.

(Clerk exits)

INNKEEPER

It'll take a little while to replace her.

STORYTELLER

We'll manage.

CHAMBERMAID

You stupid . . . senile old fool. Who do you think . . . who the fuck do you think you are? I'm not leaving. I have too much invested—I've been here too long to just give up.

STORYTELLER

You don't have a choice.

CHAMBERMAID

I'm not leaving.

STORYTELLER

It's over . . .

CHAMBERMAID

The hell it is!

STORYTELLER

Goodbye.
(*Without another thought, without another word, the Story-teller simply, calmly and unemotionally shoots her. She dies instantly.*)
(*To Handyman*) Get rid of her.

HANDYMAN

I'll put the sign back up when I'm done.

INNKEEPER

Thank you.

(*Handyman picks up Chambermaid. Exits.*)

STORYTELLER

That was easy enough.

(*Slow fade. The final image should be of the Guest, who has obviously heard the shot, rocking back and forth in terror.*)

SCENE SEVEN

(The Storyteller is seated on the sofa. The Guest enters from his room. He is obviously heading for the exit. It is late and very dark.)

STORYTELLER

Good evening.

GUEST

(Startled) Jesus!

STORYTELLER

It's very late.

GUEST

I never touched her.

STORYTELLER

(Shrugs) She says you did.

GUEST

I paid my bill.

STORYTELLER

She says you didn't.

GUEST

I'm leaving.

STORYTELLER

I couldn't allow you.

GUEST

I'm sorry. (*Heads for door.*)

STORYTELLER

So am I.

(*He raises gun, pulls back hammer. The click stops the Guest.*)

GUEST

(*Wildly*) I did not . . . I never touched her. I paid my bill . . . in advance. What more can I say? I don't understand any of this. It doesn't make any sense. I've run it through my head again and again. I did not touch her. NEVER! I never kissed her. She kissed . . . no, she never kissed me! She served me coffee. That's all! *Coffee!*

STORYTELLER

I can't let you leave.

GUEST

Why not?!

STORYTELLER

(*Shrugs*) I can't . . . that's all. Anything more . . . to give you a reason . . . would be a futile gesture. You wouldn't understand . . . you wouldn't care to understand.

GUEST

What's the point?

STORYTELLER

There isn't one. It just happened.

GUEST

Don't give me that. I can't believe . . . that's not true. I cannot believe this just happened. This is not an accident. Old men do not walk around hotel lobbies with guns.

STORYTELLER

I can't let you leave.

GUEST

I never touched her.

STORYTELLER

I'm sorry.

GUEST

I NEVER TOUCHED HER!

STORYTELLER

I cannot let you leave.

GUEST

Why not.

STORYTELLER

I've been here a long time. I can't let you leave.

GUEST

Then shoot me. *KILL ME* . . . and explain "why" to the Sheriff. Invite him over for coffee and whatever else you serve around here. Goodbye.

(*He turns to exit. The Storyteller raises the gun, aims it off to the side and fires.*)

GUEST

Shit!

STORYTELLER

I will not let you leave. Please understand that. I will shoot you, kill you and whatever else has to be done. Old men do carry guns to protect their homes. The Sheriff *will* understand that. He's been here for breakfast many times.

GUEST

You're crazy.

STORYTELLER

Sit down. (*Cocks gun*) And don't argue. I might forget what I want to say. I might just jump to the last page. Do you understand?

(The Guest sits. His eyes are fixed on the gun.)

GUEST

I haven't done a thing!

STORYTELLER

Are you sure?

GUEST

YES.

STORYTELLER

I'm not. I'm old. I stay up late; I don't sleep very well. Hell, one of the things I do—one of my pleasures—is listening to this house late at night. I know what I heard. HER MOTHER HEARD THE SAME THING!

GUEST

I just want to leave . . .

STORYTELLER

You wanted her. That's all you wanted. I SAW IT in your eyes the day you signed in. She made your choice easier. Anyone else would have left after meeting the mother. *(A brief pause)* This is a strange hotel. There is never more than one vacancy; one room to let. Yours. Our host does her best to chase new blood away. Her daughter, on the other hand, is bait. The rest of us . . . we just bet on the outcome. How long the game.

GUEST

You're crazy.

STORYTELLER

Not really. I played the game. I mastered it.

GUEST

I don't have a chance.

STORYTELLER

Maybe not. That's a matter of opinion.

GUEST

Can I leave?

STORYTELLER

No.

GUEST

I never touched her.

STORYTELLER

You're getting redundant. (*Raises gun*) She came into your room . . . with coffee . . . an extra cup . . . and . . . what else. She told you you were tired . . . told you you should rest . . . she put her hands on your shoulders . . . she massaged your neck . . . touched you. She gave you every opportunity and you took it.

GUEST

(*Rising*) NO.

STORYTELLER

You watched her undress.

GUEST

I . . .

STORYTELLER

Do you remember . . . do you remember her climbing into bed with you?

GUEST

It . . . it didn't happen that way!

STORYTELLER

Of course it did. You were there. She was there. *I was there.* I've played this game before. (*Grabs Guest by his belt.*

Holds gun in his face.) I had that little pussy—just like you. In the same way!

GUEST

You bastard . . . you fucking . . .

(*The Storyteller throws him back into the chair.*)

STORYTELLER

Welcome home.

(*He aims gun accurately and fires. Click. Nothing happens.*)

You were right. Old men don't carry guns in hotel lobbies. You can leave now. No one will stop you. We can always rent your room to someone else.

(*The Storyteller tosses the empty gun to the Guest.*)
Good night.

(*Fade out. Very slow blackout.*)

SCENE EIGHT

(*The Storyteller is alone. It is now very late.*)

STORYTELLER

That cat . . . WINDY, we called her . . . just stood there in the middle of the hallway. She wouldn't come forward—she wouldn't give way. We tried food, toys, string, anything we could think of—to coax her out. She just wouldn't budge. Finally, my father took an old corn broom and tried to sweep the cat out of the way. She pushed the broom aside, forcing my father to swing back a little harder. And then harder again. The broom would strike the animal broadside throwing it a couple of feet backwards. Each time, Windy fought back, regaining most of her lost territory. She snarled and hissed and challenged and fought my father for every inch of contested floor space. (*A brief pause*) It was a losing batle, of course. Each swipe drove her back until—eventually—she was out of the hall and locked in the bathroom. My father had successfully separated Windy from the smaller, more vulnerable cat; the cat she'd kept captive, isolated, separated from everyone else. The smaller cat, our cat, was now free . . . (*slight pause*) It was the damndest thing I'd ever seen. Our cat—the smaller one—given free choice of our entire house . . . just camped out in front of that bathroom door, mewing mournfully. We could move him, but each time, he came back. Each time it was the same . . .

(*End scene viii*)

EPILOGUE

(*The Handyman, the Clerk, the Storyteller, and The Inn-keeper are all assembled in the living room. It is a cordial, very pleasant scene.*)

STORYTELLER
(*To Innkeeper*) A bartender was a wonderful idea.

HANDYMAN
You sure found someone fast.

CLERK
I like him. He was a good choice.

INNKEEPER
Thank you.

STORYTELLER
I think he'll stay.

(*The Guest enters carrying a tray of drinks. He serves everyone ending with the Clerk. He puts the tray down, takes his own drink and leads her to the sofa. They sit together.*)

GUEST
(*To Innkeeper*) Have you rented *my old* room yet?

(*Abrupt blackout as the play ends.*)

Three: **PICNIC PUDDING**

PICNIC PUDDING
a play in three scenes

for Louis Guarino, a believer in dreams.

Cast:
John (23), a college student of no apparent ambition living in a small, Upstate New York town (near the Schroon River).

Mary (18), a very attractive, occasionally child-like, ice cream parlor soda jerk from the same town.

Jake (30), An unsightly, unpleasant, beer-belching bully from New York City.

Place:
A secluded spot along the Schroon River. Perfect for lovers . . . and hunters.

Time:
A summer afternoon.

SCENE ONE: BEFORE

(*It is noon. John is alone in the midst of a small clearing. He is an atheletic, patently handsome, thoroughly self assured young man dressed in a faded, winter flannel shirt with the sleeves cut off, a very short and tight pair of cutoffs, sweat socks and sneakers. He carries a brightly colored beach blanket and a black satchel.*)

(*As the play begins, John spreads the blanket on the ground and sits. And waits. A car horn blares in the distance.*)

JOHN

I'm down here. Hurry up.

(*He looks at his watch, mildly distressed. He waits, looking in the direction of the car, listening for the sound of someone approaching. Nothing. He looks at his watch again. There is an urgency about the time, but it is an urgency he manages to control. He shrugs and removes the watch, placing it in the satchel with methodical care. He removes a pint of rum from the bag, drinks deeply and sets the bottle aside. He then removes two rolled towels and places them, side by side, on the blanket. he takes off his shoes, brushing off his soles, and places them in the satchel. A car door slams.*)

MARY

Where are you?

JOHN

Down here. By the river. Hurry up.

(*He listens—then hears her approach. He removes his sweat socks, rolls them up and puts them in the bag.*)

MARY

[*off/whining*] How much further?

JOHN

You sound pretty close. Come on.

(*He removes his shirt, folds it carefully and packs it away in the bag. He is apparently finished at this point. He snaps the bag shut, locking it.*)
(*John listens, then lays down quickly, putting his head on one of the towels. Mary enters carrying a large, wicker picnic basket. She is dressed in a sweatshirt, zippering down the front, and a pair of gym shorts. She is obviously annoyed.*)

JOHN

It's about time . . . (*spreading his legs slightly*) I'm hungry.

MARY

(*standing over him*) So . . . eat!

(*She drops the basket directly on him and walks away. There is a child-like petulance about her.*)

JOHN

Ouch! Damnit! Why'd you . . . what the hell's wrong with you!

MARY

It's your own fault.

JOHN

What!

MARY

You broke your word.

JOHN

I did not.

MARY

LIAR!!

JOHN

I don't know what you're talking about.

MARY

That's even worse.

JOHN

Come on. Tell me what's wrong.

MARY

No.

JOHN

Come on. Please, I'm sorry . . . (*She let's him take her hands*) I mean it . . . I don't know what's wrong but . . . I don't want you mad at me. Come on . . . tell me.

MARY

It's us . . . you . . . me . . . this day. You promised me something special to make up for all the other times . . . When you were in class and I had to work. We haven't been alone in three weeks. That's a long time.

JOHN

I know.

MARY

And you promised me our own special day to make up for it.

JOHN

I know. You just said that.

MARY

And I thought you meant it.

JOHN

I did. That's why we're here. I thought you like this spot.

MARY

I love it. It's special. And I love coming back . . . with you.

JOHN

So . . . let's not fight. Okay? I love you.

(*He kisses her*)

MARY

(*her face close to his/quietly*) I don't want to share it.

JOHN

Aw . . . come on, Mary! Don't start!

MARY

I didn't start. You did.

JOHN

There was nothing I could do.

MARY

You invited *your* friend to *our* special place without even asking me.

JOHN

I haven't seen him in almost two years.

MARY

I don't care. I don't want him here. Do you understand me? (*slight pause*) This is our place and I won't have anyone else coming here. It won't be special if he comes.

JOHN

It'll always be special to me.

MARY

Well, not to me! (*pause*) I want to be *alone* with you.

JOHN

We're alone now!

MARY

For how long. You're friend is coming.

JOHN

Not for awhile, *damnit!* Look, we'll have plenty of time . . . if we don't waste it fighting. We can eat and drink and swim and do anything else you want long before he gets here. I love you.

MARY

I know. You said that already.

JOHN

I meant it. Come here. Don't fight me.

MARY

I just don't want to share you with anyone. I'm selfish, I guess.

JOHN

You're beautiful. Kiss me.

(*they kiss*)

MARY

I planned for today. I tried to think of everything that would make you happy. I care about you . . . and the way you feel. I think that's important.

JOHN

I care, too.

MARY

I'm not so sure . . . sometimes. I mean, I do everything you want and . . .

JOHN

Sometimes plans change. It can't be helped. Things happen.

MARY

Yeah . . . and everytime it does, it happens to me. I'm the one who has to take it. I'm the one who gets hurt . . . and it doesn't matter what I want.

JOHN

That's not true and you know it. I'm just as disappointed as you are. I wanted to be alone—with you—just as much . . . but it can't be helped. Jake is coming and I have to see him. He's a friend and I promised.

MARY

You promised me, too.

JOHN

This is different. Besides, he'll only be here a couple of hours. You'll meet him, share a few beers—and maybe some of that good food you cooked . . . and he'll leave. You'll never see him again. He's a friend. I want you to meet him.

MARY

If he's a real friend, he won't get in the way.

JOHN

Be nice. For me.

MARY

(*giving in*) Well . . . maybe he won't stay too long.

JOHN

That's my girl.

MARY

Maybe if he sees how happy we are, he'll just leave. I mean, three's a crowd.

JOHN

Mary.

MARY

I'll be good.

                         JOHN

Thank you.

                         MARY

I've got a surprise for you.

                         JOHN

What is it?

                         MARY

It's for later. When we go swimming.

                         JOHN

What?

                         MARY

Can't you guess?

                         JOHN

I think so . . . but I want you to tell me.

                         MARY

Well . . . I know what you like . . .

                         JOHN

Go on . . .

                         MARY

So I went to this store, you know, down town . . .

                         JOHN

Yeah . . .

                         MARY

That sells these really small bathing suits. I mean, they
are absolutely incredible. For twenty dollars, they give you
about a dime's worth of material.

                         JOHN

And you bought one . . .

MARY

Nope. I couldn't find one I liked.

JOHN

Aw, come on, Mary.

MARY

But I thought of one you'd like. And, that's the one I got.

JOHN

Let me see it.

MARY

It's just for you. I didn't do this for anyone else. When your friend comes . . .

JOHN

Mary!

MARY

I just want you to understand. He won't see it. And, as long as *he's* here, neither will you. Understand?

JOHN

Yeah. Where is it?

MARY

I'm wearing it, silly.

JOHN

Show me.

(*Mary kisses him lightly, then steps back. She begins to play with the zipper on her sweatshirt. Stops*)

MARY

No. I don't think so.

JOHN

Oh, damn! Come on.

MARY

Look for yourself.

(*John begins to unzip the sweatshirt. As he does, Mary steps closer—so that he cannot see. She takes his hand and slips it inside.*)

JOHN

Oh . . . Mary! I think you forgot something!

MARY

That's the smallest bikini I could find. Do you like it?

JOHN

You're crazy!

MARY

About you. Do you like it?

JOHN

I love it.

MARY

(*giggling*) Me, too!

(*They kiss passionately. John slips his hands into her shorts.*)

JOHN

I love all of it.

MARY

I thought you would.

(*They continue kissing . . . until Mary, with a quick push and a shove, knocks John to the ground.*)

MARY

(*laughing*) That's all you ever think of!

JOHN

What the . . .

MARY

Come on. Let's go swimming. I'll race you.

JOHN

Sure! (*getting up*) Just give me a second, okay? (*Mary starts to run*) I wanna leave Jake a note.

(*Mary stops dead in her tracks. She is suddenly furious.*)

MARY

You . . . you son-of-a-bitch! (*She zips the sweatshirt back up*) You bastard! You fucking . . .

JOHN

What is wrong now!

MARY

That's right! Leave the bastard a note! Dear Jake . . . John and Mary are down in the water . . . SKINNY DIPPING!! Come and watch! OR . . . *better yet* . . . COME AND JOIN US!!

JOHN

You're crazy!

MARY

To come here . . . today . . . YEAH! I was crazy. Well . . . BUDDY . . . no more! I'm going home.

JOHN

Come on, Mary. Cut it out. Stop acting like a . . . it's a long walk.

MARY

Don't worry about it . . . LOVER. In this suit, I'll catch a ride!

JOHN

Don't be stupid!

MARY

I am not stupid! I know who you'd rather be with! I know you don't want to be here . . . WITH ME! I know you don't care!

JOHN

I *do* care.

MARY

You called me stupid. That's not caring . . .

JOHN

(*loud*) I was talking about what you said! About HITCHING!

MARY

LIAR!!

JOHN

Stop it! Stop it . . . now! And listen, damnit! I do care . . . and I don't think you're stupid. I want you to stay . . . I mean it. Listen . . . I didn't have to come. We could have stayed in town. I could have cancelled. I wanted to come . . . to be here . . . with you.

MARY

(*looking for a way out*) I hope you . . . and your friend . . . enjoy the food. (*she starts to exit*) There's plenty.

JOHN

Please stay. I was only going to tell him to wait.

MARY

(*stopping/not looking at him*) What?

JOHN

I was going to tell him we'd be right back. So he'd wait. I didn't want him looking for us. (*slight pause*) Let's not

fight. I don't want to waste today. (*Mary nods*) Let's go
swimming.

(*Pause. Mary slowly unzips the sweatshirt and walks towards John. A few steps from him, she suddenly runs and
shouts . . .*)

MARY

Catch me!

(*exits*)
(*John watches after her. There is an inexplicable change
in his appearance. He takes the rum, drinks deeply, and
then . . .*)

JOHN

Here I come!

(*He exits as the scene ends.*)

SCENE TWO: DURING

(*The same—one hour later.*)
(*The stage is empty as Jake arrives. He is a large, unattractive man with an over-abundant beer belly. There is something about him, something instinctive, that causes strangers to shy away. His appearance, his clothing and his mannerisms do little to dispel first impression.*)
(*Jake's first action is to sneak around the campsite. He goes through the picnic basket and Mary's purse, being careful not to disturb anything. He finds a corkscrew in the basket and pockets it. He flips through the photos and cards in Mary's wallet. He counts her money, doesn't take anything, and puts everything back the way it was.*)
(*John and Mary are heard playing in the water. Then . . .*)

JOHN

[*off*] Hey! Where are you going? Give me my pants!

MARY

[*off*] Come and get 'em.

(*Laughter; spontaneous banter as they approach. Just as Mary enters, John [off] throws her sweatshirt, sopping wet, at her. It bounces off her head and lands near Jake. She is laughing and about to say something ("You . . .") when she sees Jake and freezes. Terrified. Jake picks up the shirt as Mary tries to cover herself with John's shorts. John enters.*)

JOHN

Jesus!

(*long pause*)
(*Mary hands John his pants in a quick gesture. John struggles into them.*)

JAKE

(*grinning*) Am I late . . . or just in time! (*offering the sweat-shirt to John*) I think you dropped this.

JOHN

(*giving it to Mary*) I'm sorry.
(*He wraps himself in a towel. Tosses the other to Mary.*)
(*to Jake*) Your timing sucks.

JAKE

You mean, I'm too early! Well . . . hell . . . I can't say I'm too sorry about that . . . but it wasn't my fault. I was anxious to see you. I guess I got here extra fast.

MARY

(*shaken*) Is he . . .

JOHN

Yeah . . . well . . . eh . . . it's not exactly the way I wanted you two to meet but . . . eh . . . Jake, this is Mary.

JAKE

I know. You said she was a beauty. The evidence didn't lie.

MARY

He . . . my god! You could have told me.

JOHN

What's wrong?

MARY

I thought he . . . we . . .

JAKE

I see you told her about me.

MARY

I thought we were . . . you know . . . dead . . . raped . . . and . . .

JAKE

(*grinning to John*) You really did tell her about me.
(*to Mary*) You had nothing to worry about. He's the one
with the cute buns.

JOHN

Cut it out.

MARY

(*still shaken*) He should have told me.

JAKE

It wasn't necessary. I mean, I was going to meet you
anyway.

MARY

And you! You heard us coming. You could have said something.

JAKE

I didn't want to spoil your fun. Besides, I'd just gotten here
myself.

MARY

Oh?

JOHN

How about a beer?

JAKE

Sure! I can use a quick one . . . before I go.

JOHN

What's the hurry? (*a quick look at Mary*) You can eat with
us.

JAKE

Hell, man, I just stopped by to say hello. Besides, I can see
you're tied down for awhile. I'd be in the way.

JOHN

Bull. We want you to stay. Both of us.

(*after a pause*)

MARY

Sure. John told me you were coming. I mean, you haven't seen each other in awhile. And that other thing was an accident.

JAKE

You could say that.

MARY

Don't worry about it.

JAKE

I won't.

MARY

Then you'll stay?

JAKE

For a little while. My momma told me never to be a nuisance. Especially to friends.

MARY

Good. Then it's settled.

JAKE

I've got some grub in the car. I'll get it and be right back.

MARY

We have plenty.

JAKE

That's all right. I like *to share*. Be right back.

JOHN

Need any help.

JAKE

No. Stay with Mary.

(*he exits*)

JOHN

Thank you.

MARY

I did it for you ... like always. He's your friend and I wasn't about to be rude. But, don't get the wrong idea. We invited him to eat—and that's all. When he gets back, we eat. Then it's goodbye to ol' Jake. I won't be polite to that peeping Tom again.

JOHN

That was an accident.

MARY

You could say that.

JOHN

What do you think?

MARY

Of him! Goddamnit, John, don't get me started! He's a pig! A fat, ugly, mother-fucking pig ...

JOHN

Mary ...

MARY

I don't know how you and he could possibly be friends and I don't care. I don't like him! I am mad as hell he saw me with my tits hanging out and I do not want him here!!

JOHN

Jesus ... come on ...

MARY

I won't ruin your precious little reunion. I promised! But, you remember what I said. You eat up and get him the hell on his way or, I swear, I'll leave. I'll hit that road and I'll hitch my ass back to town . . . and I don't care who sees my tits on the way!

JOHN

He'll be gone before you know it. I promise.

MARY

Just get rid of him.

JOHN

I'm sorry about before.

MARY

You told me.

JOHN

I just want you to know I mean it.

MARY

I know.

JOHN

I'm sorry about today, too. (*no answer*) I don't want to fight. I love you.

MARY

I love you, too.

JOHN

Let's kiss and make up.

MARY

Let's get the food out. (*smiles*) We can kiss later.

JOHN

Okay, then . . . let's go for the record! Dishes, knives, forks, chicken, potato salad, napkins . . . what else . . . apple pie . . .

MARY

Leave that in the basket . . . for later.

JOHN

Okay . . . fruit . . . beer . . . chips . . . and . . . and . . . I think that's it. Did we forget anything?

MARY

Just a change of clothes. I'm freezing.

JOHN

I can warm you up.

MARY

I bet you can.

JOHN

Come on. Let me try. That's it. I'll just rub my hands over your arms . . . like this. Better? And wrap my arms around you . . . and share the warmth. I'm not cold at all. How's that feel. Does it excite you? Mmmm! I think it does!

MARY

Don't be so damn proud of yourself. I'm just cold.

JOHN

I'm sorry.

MARY

I know. (*pause*) Thank you. (*pause*) Mmmmm . . . I think you're right.

JAKE

[*off*] I don't wanna suprise you again . . . so put back whatever it is you're playing with. Here I come.

JOHN

Hurry up. We're starved.

MARY

Cut his food, if you have to.

JOHN

This won't take long.

MARY

Good. I don't like him at all.

JOHN

When you get to know him . . . never mind.
(*Mary starts making the plates*)
I'll get the beers. (*he opens three*) Hey, fatso, hurry up.
We've got food waiting.

JAKE

[*off*] Well, why didn't you say so. (*enters*) I'm here! Let's eat.
(*He has a large hero which he unceremoniously cuts into
three sections with a large folding knife.*
Now we can all share.
(*He takes a plate and—gluttonously—adds to it*)
You need one of these where I come from.

MARY

(*innocently*) That's too bad.

JAKE

Not really. It's part of the job.

JOHN

Jake's in building maintenance.

JAKE

Security, I got promoted.

JOHN

Is that good?

JAKE

If I live.

MARY

Why would anyone . . .

JAKE

It has its advantages. My company owns four buildings on the west side and they want 'em torn down. There's a big money project coming. *Big Money!* And I stand to make some of it . . . if I can get those damn wreckers in on time.

MARY

That doesn't sound so dangerous.

JAKE

Maybe not . . . but, there are still people living there. I have to move 'em out and lock their apartments. And keep 'em locked. That's the hard part.

JOHN

Squatters.

JAKE

Junkie scum mostly. That's where the knife comes in. (*to Mary*) Those bastards have more ways of breakin' in than I have of stopping 'em. Only it's my job to keep 'em out . . . or kick 'em out. And that ain't easy . . . or safe. It's sorta like fucking a sleeping lion. You try not to wake her up. (*laughs*) You've gotta be careful . . . or damned lucky . . . to stay alive.

JOHN

I know your stories. Should we stop eating?

JAKE

(*to Mary*) That depends . . . are you squeamish?

MARY

. . . eh . . . no . . . not really . . .

JAKE

So ... eat! (*slight pause*) Now, I have to tell you ... I'm used to these people. I know how slick they can be ... I don't suprise easy ... but ... even so ... you gotta watch 'em ... or they'll trick ya. Like yesterday. I stumbled on a whole room of 'em. Eight of 'em—with mattresses, no less! And I didn't even know they were there. I just walked in and almost fell over one of 'em.

MARY

What'd you do?

JAKE

I broke open a window and rolled 'em out!

JOHN

(*laughing*) You're kidding!

MARY

Won't they come back?

JAKE

I doubt it. We were six stories up at the time.

MARY

Oh ... my ... god ...

JAKE

You're not eating.

MARY

You ...

JAKE

What did ya expect? I couldn't tell my boss eight shooters broke in—*with mattresses*—and set up housekeeping. I'd blow my bonus.

MARY

That's disgusting! How can you brag about ... eight ...

JAKE

Junkies.

JOHN

She doesn't know you the way I do. (*to Mary*) I wouldn't believe a word this guy says. He's a natural born liar.

(*Jake makes a whistling sound to indicate someone falling.*)

JAKE

Splat!

JOHN

He loves to make up stories.

JAKE

That's right. I made it up.

JOHN

And he loves to tease.

MARY

You're terrible!

JAKE

You shouldn't say that. We haven't been to bed, yet!

MARY

John!

JOHN

Don't let him bother you. I told you he likes to tease.

MARY

Well I don't like it. Make him stop.

JAKE

He knows me too well for that.

MARY

(*anger mounting*) Well I don't know you at all!

JAKE

He must have told you something.

MARY

Only that you were friends . . .

JAKE

And you can't believe that?

MARY

No . . . I mean . . . I don't understand it . . . you're so different.

JAKE

That's true. But we do have something in common. Didn't he tell you how we met?

JOHN

No!

JAKE

It's a good story.

(*Long pause. John shakes his head. Mary looks at John.*)

MARY

I have to admit, I'm curious.

JAKE

It's no big deal, really. We just happened to meet, sorta by accident—and we hit it off. We talked for almost twelve straight hours and we've been getting together—on and off—ever since. I've known him . . . what . . . almost four years now.

MARY

(*disappointed*) Oh.

JAKE

The fact we were in jail at the time shouldn't surprise you.

JOHN

Jake!

JAKE

(*to John*) There's nothing to be embarrassed about. The charges were dropped, weren't they? (*to Mary*) He was in for twelve hours before they let him go; I was there for three months.

MARY

Why?

JAKE

I beat up a tenant. (*looking at Mary*) The bum woke me up at one in the morning—complaining about a roach in his bed. The guy was a real nut. I mean, he's foaming at the mouth and ranting and raving about filthy roaches running all over the place . . . which, you've got to know, is an insane exaggeration. I mean, we have roaches. Every building in New York has roaches . . . even on Park Avenue! But, we also have exterminators. They weren't running all over the place. But, even if they were, who cares! It's one o'clock in the morning . . . and I'm off duty. I don't want to be bothered, so I try to get rid of the guy . . . with a joke, you know. I tell him he's not allowed to have pets . . . it's in the lease . . . and I laugh. And that drives the guy crazy. The jerk starts yelling and screaming. He tries to wake the whole building up—to turn them against me, too! He's cursing at me—saying all sorts of bad things, lying left and right like a mother fucker. I mean, hell, what am I supposed to do. I punched him. I knocked him down hard. He stopped yelling. (*slight pause*) I don't like yelling. I told the judge that. He gave me three months, anyway. But, by then, John and I were friends. He was there when they let me out.

MARY

(*to John*) Why were you in jail?

JAKE

It was a sex charge, wasn't it?

JOHN

Jake, that's enough! Don't start!

JAKE

He was in college, by then, majoring in pussy. I mean, skirts were the only reason he went. He spent all his time hanging around the dorms—picking up anything that moved.

JOHN

Cut it out!!

JAKE

Two guards found him—alone—in one of the girl's rooms. She was in class at the time. All the girl's clothing was piled on her bed. John was on top of them when they caught him. All *his* clothes were on the floor!

MARY

I don't wanna hear anymore.

JAKE

There isn't much more. His father worked things out. The charges were dropped. The school asked him to leave and, after awhile, they moved up here.

JOHN

You son-of-a-bitch! You fucking . . . Mary . . . it's not true! None of it. He's lying! I told you he likes to make things up. (*yelling*) TELL HER!!

JAKE

You're ruining a good story.

MARY

(*quiet*) Is it true?

JAKE

I tell stories. Some are true. Some . . . (*shrugs*)

> ### JOHN
> (*desperate*) I was arrested for drunk driving. My father paid the bills. I was out in a few hours. Period!

> ### MARY
> (*to Jake*) I don't like you.

> ### JOHN
> (*yelling*) What the hell's wrong with you! You son . . . of . . . a . . . bitch! We're friends! We're supposed to be friends! I invited you here to have a few beers and some laughs and all of a sudden you go crazy on us! You try to fuck me up with my girl. You were deliberately rude and obnoxious and . . . you're acting like a crazy-sick mother fucker!!

> ### JAKE
> *STOP YELLING AT ME!!!*
>
> (*pause*)

> ### JOHN (*quiet*)
> I'm not gonna fight. It's not worth it.

> ### JAKE
> *Don't yell at me!*

> ### JOHN
> I'm sorry. I won't.

> ### JAKE
> (*quieting down*) I told you . . . I don't like it when people yell . . .

> ### JOHN
> Okay. Just relax . . . sit down.

> ### MARY
> (*timid*) Maybe you should leave.

> ### JAKE
> (*very quiet*) Yeah, you're right. Maybe I should. I'm sorry.

                    JOHN

It's okay.

                    JAKE

I'll keep in touch.

                    JOHN

Sure.

                    JAKE

It's been a bad week . . . with the junkies and all.

(*exits*)

                    MARY

Are you alright?

                    JOHN

Yeah.

                    MARY

I don't ever want to see him again.

                    JOHN

You don't have to.
(*long pause*)
Why don't you clean this stuff up? I'll be right back.

                    MARY

Where are you going?

                    JOHN

I just want to square things with Jake.

                    MARY

Why? (*!*)

                    JOHN

He's a friend. I just want to tell him to call me. To keep in touch.

MARY

He knows that.

JOHN

I want to be sure. Jake's a funny guy.

MARY

I know.

JOHN

I won't bring him back with me.

MARY

I don't like it.

JOHN

You don't know Jake. He's rude and vulgar and mean sometimes . . . but most of what he does is like his stories. They're for effect. They keep you from looking too deep . . . most people he keeps at a distance. I like the man. I value his friendship.

MARY

John . . .

JOHN

I'll be right back. I have plans for today. (*He reaches for her zipper and lowers it a little*) And, *you* are a part of them.

MARY

Hurry up.

JOHN

Clean up. I'll be right back for dessert.

(*he exits*)

MARY

(*softly*) Hurry up.

(*She starts repacking the basket as the scene ends.*)

SCENE THREE: AFTER

(The same . . . fifteen minutes later. Mary is still repacking the basket as Jake enters.)

JAKE

I'm supposed to apologize.

MARY

(startled) Oh . . . Jesus! Where's John.

JAKE

He's back there . . . giving me a chance to show you I'm sorry.

MARY

It's alright. John explained it to me.

JAKE

Really? What did he say?

MARY

Nothing much . . . only you were a nice guy and you had a bad day.

JAKE

He didn't say I was rude and vulgar and told stories to cover up?

MARY

What?

JAKE

It doesn't matter.

MARY

John!

JAKE

I just want you to know how sorry I am . . . ruining your "special" day the way I did.

MARY

John!!

JAKE

He won't answer you.

MARY

Why not?

JAKE

That's another story.

MARY

John . . . where are you!

JAKE

He came up the path—looking for me . . . like he said he would. I stopped just past those trees. I wasn't ready to leave yet . . . so it didn't take him long to find me. He was very upset—about the way things turned out. About *you* asking me to leave. About yelling . . .

MARY

Where is he?

JAKE

He left. He said he was sorry. He said my friendship was important to him. He said you didn't want me around. He said you wanted to start a fight . . .

MARY

That's not true . . .

JAKE

To get rid of me. He said you told him you never wanted to see me again. I heard you say it. It wasn't nice. He said he was sorry. I walked him to his car, we shook hands and he left.

MARY

I don't believe you. Where is he? John! *JOHN!*

JAKE

Don't yell (*slight pause*) I told you. It was a story. One of *my* stories. And, a lie. (*very matter-of-fact*) I killed him.

MARY

(*terrified*) Stop teasing me.

JAKE

(*pulling a gun*) I'm not. He yelled at me. And he followed me. I used my knife on him . . . so I need this now. The knife is still in him.

MARY

What . . . do . . .

JAKE

Sit down. Please.

MARY

What do you want?

JAKE

To talk. To apologize.

MARY

You don't have to.

JAKE

I know. I gave you the wrong impression. I'm sorry.

MARY

Where's John.

JAKE

He turned against me. He called me rude and vulgar and . . . what was it . . . mean. I am not mean. No. I tell stories —to my friends—because they like them. They ask me to tell them. That's the truth. He shouldn't have made fun of me. It wasn't nice. I've done a lot for him. Did you know that? When he was in jail, I listened to him. He cried. He said he was scared—because the guards would tell his father what he'd done. It was true—the story I told you. He'd broken into that girl's room . . . because she wasn't interested. She wouldn't even look at him. He waited until she went to class, you know, and he broke into her room. He took all of her clothes, her dresses and her underwear and her stockings and he covered the bed with them. And then, he took off his own clothes and climbed into bed with her. Do you understand? He didn't want her to say no. He was on top of her trying to make her love him. The guards heard him and they caught him. He was screwing this great mountain of clothing—moaning and screaming and begging her to love him. He kept begging even after they dragged him out of there. And, then, he was in jail—with me. He told me everything—even about his father. The old man paid some money to the girl, you know, and the school and they let him out. That's why they came here. The father doesn't know about me. John never told him. I wanted you to know the truth.

MARY

Where's John?

JAKE

He's in the bushes. Over there. I pushed him under it and covered him with needles. I'm sorry things didn't work out. (*pause*) Am I forgiven?

MARY

What . . . eh . . . yes.

JAKE

Good.

MARY

What do you want?

JAKE

To try again, of course. We were supposed to have a picnic.

MARY

Can you put the gun away?

JAKE

No. Can I have a beer?

MARY

. . . eh . . . yeah . . . sure . . .

JAKE

Good. Thank you. (*he drinks it down in one gulp*) Wanna go swimming.

MARY

What!

JAKE

John told me about your suit. I'd like to see it, too.

MARY

NO!

JAKE

You're my friend now. Friends share everything.

MARY

(*whining*) I don't want to . . .

JAKE
(*cocks gun*) Please. Stand up. Now.

(*Mary stands. Hesitates. He waves the gun slightly. She unzips the shirt.*)

Thank you. (*He walks over to her*) John told me this was a special day for you.

(*He lifts her head with the gun so that she is looking at him.*)

I didn't want to kill him. He said, "no".

(*He slowly slides the sweatshirt open and off her shoulders —using the gun. He works the shirt down her arms and off.*)

I'll make it up to you. This *will* be a special day.

MARY
Please.

JAKE
You're my friend, right?

MARY
Yes.

JAKE
Good. Kiss me.

(*He takes her face in both hands—pressing the gun against her cheek—and moves her into position. He kisses her as she stands there limply. At some point, he lowers the hand w/out the gun behind her back and holds her tightly. He raises the hand with the gun, still kissing her, and sud-denly—violently—strikes her in the head. She is knocked unconcious. He lowers her onto the blanket.*)
(*John, dressed in a suit, enters and watches. Jake kneels over her and rips her shorts away in a slow, controlled, very deliberate motion.*)

JOHN

That was some performance.

JAKE

I get my money's worth.

JOHN

Everything alright?

JAKE

So far.

(*Jake puts the sweatshirt and the torn shorts in the picnic basket. Closes it.*)

JOHN

I'll take the basket and my bag. Make sure you clean everything else.

JAKE

I know the routine.

JOHN

Good.

JAKE

Anything else.

JOHN

Next time—use a different story.

JAKE

Just adding a little realism.

JOHN

Change it!

JAKE

Okay.

JOHN

I've got to get back to the campus.

JAKE

I owe you.

JOHN

I'll send you a bill.

(*exits*)

(*slow blackout as Jake, standing over Mary, begins to unbuckle his pants.*)

(*the end*)

Four: SLIGHT IRREGULARS

SLIGHT IRREGULARS
a play in one act with an epilogue

In Memory of "POE"

Cast:
Gladys, the office go-fer
Harvey, a scientist
Ellen, his new assistant

Place:
The reception area of a commercial laboratory.

Time:
Today.

(Virtual darkness. Gladys is sitting on a stool facing the audience. Harvey, facing away, watches a screen.)
(Harvey and Gladys speak simultaneously.)

HARVEY

(As Harvey speaks, a series of slides are projected on the screen. They are all front, side and rear view, full length nudes. He speaks in a hushed tone, as if to a recorder.) Model six-thirty-eight: Male. Subject is six foot two and one third inches tall. Weight: 180 lbs. Hair: Brown. Eyes: Brown. Approximate age: Twenty. Good muscle tone. Athletic structure. Intelligence quotient: Undetermined. Model six-thirty-nine: Female. Subject height: 5'4" Weight: 100 lbs. Hair: Blonde. Eyes: Blue. Approximate age: Eighteen. Good muscle tone. Dance/gymnastics design. Intelligence: Undetermined. Model six-forty: male. 6'3" and ¾" tall. Weight: 200 lbs. Hair: Brown. Eyes: Hazel. Approxi-

GLADYS

This is one weird place to work, let me tell you. I mean, they got nothing but nudies—men and women—all over the place. Oh, I don't mean the workers—I don't take my clothes off for nobody. Unh-uh! It ain't in my contract. I mean the patients—or whatever they are. None of 'em wears a lick of clothes. Ever! And they got this doctor who spends all his time looking at nudie pictures—writing things down, measuring this thing and that thing and just sorta getting real bleary eyed about the whole thing. He's my boss and the guy in charge, too—which explains a lot about everything. I mean, he's some kinda weird scientist that's got his own secret laboratory right up stairs. I ain't allowed to go in so I don't know what he's got going on in there—and I don't want to know! Not with all the nudies around.

(quietly) Now, don't get me wrong. They ain't bad—none of them—so I ain't worried. Just curious. The nudies don't bother no one. They don't do much of anything, really. The doc's got

mate age: 35 years. Under developed muscle tone. Sedentary program. Intelligence: Undetermined. Subject six-forty-one: Male. *(the next three slides are blank)* Where is # 641? *(a fourth click—a female)* Model 6-42: Female. *(back four)* Model 6-40: male. Where is # 641? WHERE!

GLADYS!!

this room, in the basement, where he keeps them—men and women all together—and they don't do nothin'! I clean up in there every day and its always the same. Men and women, all of 'em naked, like I said—all types and shapes, good lookin' ones, too—just sittin' around not doin' *nothin'*, not lookin' at *nothin'*, not even talkin! It's like they ain't alive. But, I see them breathing so I know. . .

It's weird. But they pay real good. And I got plenty to do . . . to keep from getting bored. I mean, anything goes wrong—that's my job. I like my job.

SHIT!

(Gladys stops talking and rushes into the light of the slide projector.)

GLADYS

Yes, sir!

HARVEY

I'm missing model 6-41. Have you seen it?

GLADYS

Unh-uh! I can't see nothin' right now.

HARVEY

Sorry.

(Blackout. Lights fade up.)

GLADYS

Oh, my! Now I can't see nothin' but spots. What's missing?

HARVEY

6-41: "All American Male".

GLADYS

I haven't seen him. Have you checked the file?

HARVEY

It's missing.

GLADYS

I don't know. He should be there. I can look.

HARVEY

#6-41. Male: 6'3". Weight: 175. Eyes: hazel. Hair: Auburn. Classic American profile.

GLADYS

I haven't seen him. I'd remember. (*a thought*) What are you saying, anyway? I didn't take him. Unh-uh! I don't take nothin'. You should know that. Besides, what would I do with *pictures*. I've got a husband, a five-foot-seven, 280 lb, all-American beer drinking man. He *wouldn't* understand.

HARVEY

(*out of control*) I don't know what's going on around here. I just don't know. This is a laboratory, for Chrissake! I should be able to find *records*. I can't find anything I want . . . *and the project's behind schedule.* I need those photos!

GLADYS

That new assistant of yours, Ellen, might know. She's been in the files. She's had her hands on everything.

HARVEY

Hell! I can't go tracking her down, too. I'm overdue in the lab. Can you get her for me?

GLADYS

Right away, sir.

HARVEY

Good. I'll be right back!

(*he exits*)

GLADYS

Pictures! I gotta be crazy. If she don't have 'em . . . they're lost. And if they're lost, I'm gonna spend all day looking for slides he wants but doesn't need. (*picks up phone*) He knows them all by heart. He'll just look at them for a second and start writing the same . . . hello, Ellen . . . yeah . . . could you come in here? The doc needs you. Thanks. (*thinks*) Not that I wouldn't mind a little all-American nudie around the house. (*shakes head*) But it wouldn't be worth the . . . (*thinks: the thought interests her for a moment. Then . . .*) Unh-uh! If my husband knew what I've been looking at all day . . . I mean the men . . . I'd be in for one serious dose of pain. No sir, it just ain't worth it.

ELLEN

(*entering*) What's up?

(*She is an attractive woman, about thirty, dressed outlandishly in a lab coat and fishnet stockings. Gladys seems surprised by the outfit.*)

GLADYS

Doc's missing a file.

ELLEN

Which one?

GLADYS

. . . eh . . . 641. What're you dressed up for?

ELLEN

This! It's the new uniform. Do you like it?

GLADYS

I ain't wearing one.

ELLEN

I don't think it's for you. It's for the medical staff. Did you get a memo?

GLADYS

No.

ELLEN

There . . . you see. I just got mine with a memo from Doc Harvey. It's a perfect fit.

GLADYS

He's good at measuring things.

ELLEN

I like it.

GLADYS

641?

ELLEN

What?

GLADYS

Doc's missing file. #641.

(*Ellen looks through her clip board.*)

ELLEN

We don't have a 6-41.

GLADYS

Doc seems to think so. "6′3″, 175 lbs, All American Profile".

ELLEN

I can check the files . . .

(*She does so as Harvey enters.*)

HARVEY

Well?

GLADYS

She's checking.

ELLEN

We don't have a model 641.

HARVEY

Of course we do. I put it together myself . . . a male, 6'3"
tall, weight: 175, eyes: hazel, hair: auburn . . .

GLADYS

"Classic All-American Profile".

ELLEN

That model was discontinued.

HARVEY

That's impossible. When?

ELLEN

I'm not sure. I received a memo . . .

HARVEY

I didn't get any damn memo! 6-41 was a recent model.

ELLEN

We lost 6-41, 3-88 and 11-59 all at the same time.

HARVEY

They're all recent models!

ELLEN

I'm afraid so.

HARVEY

How am I supposed to complete the project without inventory? (*silence*) Oh, hell . . . we'd better get back to work.
Gladys, go up to lab . . .

GLADYS

Unh-uh! I ain't allowed.

HARVEY

I give you permission.

GLADYS

It's not in my contract.

HARVEY

Your contract says you work for me.

GLADYS

I don't like it.

HARVEY

Consider it a promotion. I'll see you get a raise.

GLADYS

Yes, sir! What do I do? I mean, I ain't trained for the lab.

HARVEY

Just take model 8-17—the female one—down to the basement.

GLADYS

Then what?

HARVEY

Come back. And, be careful. Get help if you need it. 8-17 is our largest model. Over 210 lbs.

GLADYS

A fat nudie!

HARVEY

We manipulated the thyroid. It was an experiment.

GLADYS

That don't surprise me. I'll make sure she has plenty of room down there. (*exiting*) A fat nudie! What a day!

HARVEY

They're going to terminate the project.

ELLEN

They can't.

HARVEY

What else can they do?

ELLEN

But . . .

HARVEY

I think they've already started. I'm just guessing, mind you. It's not official . . . I haven't received a memo . . . *I don't get memos anymore* . . . but what else makes sense. They've discontinued our latest models. We have orders and requests we can't fill. Our product still doesn't work; our inventory just sits in the basement. It doesn't do anything. It doesn't move . . .

ELLEN

We have plenty of spare parts . . .

HARVEY

It doesn't matter. The parts fit together just fine. They always have. But something goes wrong—I don't know what—*after* we're finished. They're irregulars. I don't know why. I don't have the answers and the people upstairs are tired of waiting. It's a matter of image now.

ELLEN

We have customers!

HARVEY

Millions of them! And each and every one has a special request, a special need, a unique design change that we cannot satisfy. It's more than money now; it's bad for the corporate image. They'll get out of the market . . . close us down . . .

ELLEN

But . . . I just got my uniform!

HARVEY

Oh! It came! I'm sorry. I didn't notice My mind's been . . .

ELLEN

It's okay.

HARVEY

I'm glad you got to wear it. At least something works around here.

ELLEN

(*hesitant*) No one else got one.

HARVEY

It was just for you . . . as my assistant.

ELLEN

Why thank you! That was very considerate. I like it.

HARVEY

I picked it out myself.

ELLEN

You have wonderful taste.

HARVEY

Thank you. Does it fit?

ELLEN

Perfectly. (*suddenly uneasy*) Doesn't it?

HARVEY

I don't know. Let me see. (*He examines her somewhat personally*) Yes, the shoulders seem to fit. And the arms. Yes. The length is good. And the overall shape fits you just right. Yes. Everything is fine. It works. It is just what I had in mind.

ELLEN

I'm glad.

HARVEY

I'm sorry you won't get to wear it for long. We don't have that much time left.

ELLEN

(*uneasy*) There's still *some* time . . .

HARVEY

You've only been here a short while. I hoped we could get to know each other better . . .

ELLEN

Doctor . . .

HARVEY

Come up to the lab with me. Right now. We can work on an experiment . . . together. Please.
(*He begins to unbutton her lab coat.*)
We can work it out. I promise. Ellen?

ELLEN

I'm sorry. I don't . . .

HARVEY

Consider it a promotion.

(*He kisses her passionately. She begins to respond, then, inexplicibly, drops her arms to her side. She just stands there, staring blankly ahead. She appears totally devoid of energy and emotion.*)

ELLEN

I'm sorry . . .

(*She sits with a thud.*)

HARVEY

Ellen! This isn't funny! Ellen . . . talk to me! I insist you talk to me! Damnit! I don't have to take this. I'm in charge here. Talk! Move! DO SOMETHING! Damn you . . .

(*He slaps her just as Gladys enters. Ellen exhibits no change in expression; no response.*)

GLADYS

Whoa!!

HARVEY

It's all right.

GLADYS

It doesn't look alright to me.

HARVEY

It was an experiment. (*slight pause/defeated*) I'd like you to take Ellen to the basement.

GLADYS

Her, too?

HARVEY

Yes.

GLADYS

If you say so. Ellen, you wanna go now?

HARVEY

You'll have to help her.

GLADYS

If it ain't one thing . . . let's go.

HARVEY

Put her uniform in the closet when you're done.

GLADYS

Whatever.

HARVEY

Do you know what we do here?

GLADYS

No one ever told me.

HARVEY

We build people.

GLADYS

That don't surprise me. This is a weird place.

HARVEY

When you get back I'll tell you all about it.

GLADYS

Is this another promotion?

HARVEY

If you like.

GLADYS

I won't take my clothes off. It's not in my contract.

HARVEY

I know.

GLADYS

Good. I'll be right back.
(*She takes Ellen by the hand and talks to her as if she were a baby being taught to walk.*)
That's it. One step at a time. You can do it . . . that's it . . . that's it. One step at a time. There we go . . . (*exits*)

HARVEY

I don't understand it. They just won't move.
(*the phone rings*)
Yeah . . . okay . . . I'll be right up. No, I wasn't doing anything important.

(*As he exits, blackout . . .*)

EPILOGUE

(The same. Gladys returns to an empty room.)

GLADYS

Now where'd he go. He's supposed to tell me about my new job.

(the phone rings)

Hello . . . no . . . the doc ain't here . . . oh . . . I see . . . he don't work here anymore. That doesn't surprise me . . . yeah . . . he was going to tell me about that. Do I still get the promotion . . . yeah . . . you're kidding . . . no . . . I can do that . . . yeah . . . whatever you say . . . sure . . . bye!

(She hangs up and dials quickly)

There have been strange days and weird days . . . but this . . . this . . . I don't have a word for this. This goes . . . hello, honey . . . you're not going to believe this . . . yeah, *I'm at work* . . . that's why I'm calling . . . I just got two promotions in one day . . . and my boss got fired. I'm in charge now. I'm the boss now. *(annoyed)* Yeah . . . that's right! *I'm the only one left.* Doc's gone and I just dumped Ellen in the basement. Anything else? Yeah . . . I'll be making more money! *A lot more money!* I'll tell you about it when I get home.

(She hangs up quickly. Looks around.)

I can run a place like this.

(Gladys picks up the slide projector control and starts running it)

If they would only move . . . *(looks at the phone)* I'd get a trade in . . .

(Darkness. The pictures continue, ending with Ellen, Doc and . . .)*
(The play is over.)

* If multiple projectors are available, the finale should be presented as a front, side and rear-view chorus line of slight irregulars.

Five: **IT NEVER SNOWS ON MARDI GRAS
IN TAHITI**

IT NEVER SNOWS ON MARDI GRAS IN TAHITI
a play in four scenes with an epilogue

For Aldo Del Sorbo, who laughs

Cast:
Gary (30), the soon-to-be evicted writer
Mike (40), his new midwestern neighbor

Place:
An old Manhattan apartment. At present, it is in the process of being transformed into a scene from the South Pacific. Piles of sand litter the floor. A Tahitian hut stands partially constructed in a corner. Piles of driftwood, palm fronds and coconuts are scattered around the room.

SCENE ONE

(*The room is empty but the lights are on. Polynesian music is heard, occasionally mixed with the noise of street traffic. After a moment, there is the sound of a minor crash on the stairs [off] followed by a few spontaneous expletives. And then . . .*)

GARY

[*off*] I won't miss these steps—not a damn one of them—I can tell you that! Hey, super—Mr. Invisible Man—how about a light bulb before I leave! Make it my going away present.

(*He enters carrying a case of live crabs. He is winded from the climb.*)

Six unending, unyielding, untended, uneven, unnatural, never-get-used-to-'em flights of mother-fucking steps and that son-of-a-bitch makes you climb in the dark. I'm leaving . . . OKAY . . . buy a bulb!

(*There is a pounding from below. Gary gets a hammer and pounds back several times—loudly!*)

I can keep it up as long as you can, you crazy bastard! It doesn't bother me.

(*He checks the box of crabs*)

Hey, those crabs are alive—so be careful. Don't hurt them!

(*He begins to undress to his jockey shorts*)

It is small wonder people feel isolated in this town. I mean . . . hell . . . you push and poke and punish someone long enough, you make the take-it-for-granted easy shit impossible and sooner or later they are going to pull back into ol' mother nature's great protective shell. You frustrate 'em until they got to get away. Got to! I mean, to survive. It's kind of like exile. Isolation. A world of personal protection zones—lots of dead layers to keep the dangers away. Lots of lonely people in this town. Lots of turtles in their shells. Lots of zombies. (*slight pause*) Can't run away and stay put. Hurts too much. When you go—you're gone. No once more, over the shoulder, last glance at the ol' homestead, home-sick bullshit. It's goodbye, so long, I'm going . . . gone! Poof!

(*He wraps himself in traditional Tahitian garb.*)

And, I'm gone. One more scene and it's out the door, hit the road time. Bye-Bye! Poof!

(*Mike steps into the doorway*)

MIKE

I think this belongs to you.

(*He holds up a squirming crab, just a little afraid of it.*)

GARY

Beware strangers bearing crabs.

MIKE

Excuse me?

GARY

A cheap joke. Ignore me. (*an after thought*) Or laugh. The people who know me—friends and other animals—just laugh.

MIKE

Oh!

GARY

For god sakes, come in . . . unless you're waiting for a re-ward or a good night kiss. Both are out of the question.

MIKE

(*entering*) I just want to return your . . .

GARY

I don't know you.

MIKE

I'm just moving in. (*looking around*) I was behind you on the stairs. I heard you fall.

GARY

And you brought one of my little pets home. That's very kind. Thank you.

MIKE

I heard you say you dropped one . . .

GARY

Maybe several. I haven't counted. But thanks, anyway. It was a big help. I mean . . . they insist on their afternoon walk . . . but they're not very good on the stairs. Arthritis!

MIKE

Oh . . . I . . . uh . . . see . . . uh!

GARY

I only adopt handicapped pets.

MIKE

That's very . . .

GARY

Thank you. You can put him in that box with the rest of his unfortunate family.

MIKE

Fine . . . uh . . . you have a couple of dozen!

GARY

I don't mind the extra work. Besides, it would be cruel to split them up. I wouldn't feel right.

MIKE

I see . . . well . . . I have to be going. Lots of work . . . un-packing . . .

GARY

I still don't know who you are. Other than the basics.

MIKE

Basics?

GARY

You're a foreigner. I'm not being racial . . . but you are not from New York. Probably mid-western. Definitely rural. Nebraska, maybe. You were born *by* 1942, tend to prefer simple foods—probably vegetarian, hence the slight physique—and dislike strenuous exercise. I bet there's a lot of sagging muscle beneath that loose clothing. Oh . . . and you don't laugh.

MIKE

(*with anger*) For your information, since you seem so curious, I'm from Wisconsin. Milwaukee, Wisconsin—a city. I am in *this* city because my employer made an unfortunate decision and sent me here! I was born in '43, am a gourmet chef and run ten miles a day . . . so you can forget about my muscle tone!

GARY

(*amused*) I haven't given it a second thought.

MIKE

And, when something is funny, I laugh!

GARY

Too bad. I enjoy the sound.

MIKE

Now . . . if you'll excuse me.

GARY

Don't leave because of a few bad parlor games. That only worked for Basil Rathbone in all those old Sherlock Holmes movies. Besides, you missed the point.

MIKE

What point?

GARY

Gary.

MIKE

What?

GARY

Gary. My name. One of the *basics* you left out.

MIKE

Oh . . . uh . . . uh . . . Mike . . .

GARY

Hello.

MIKE

. . . uh . . . hello.

GARY

I'm pleased to meet you.

MIKE

. . . uh . . . yeah . . . me, too.

GARY

I hope you'll enjoy the building.

MIKE

I'm sure I will.

GARY

Good.
(*silence*)
I don't know about you, but I found the bit with the crab
a lot more interesting. That last bit was . . . well . . . *boring.*

MIKE

(*perhaps, a smile*) Sorry.

GARY

Don't be. Or, at least, don't admit it. Mistakes are rarely
tolerated in these parts.

MIKE

I wasn't apologizing.

GARY

Good. And stop looking so scared. That could be fatal. Remember where you are.

MIKE

Do you always talk like this?

GARY

Constantly. I come from a long line of chronic chatterers. We fill the void, so to speak. This is a very hyperactive, hypertense, shout to be heard, shove to be seen, drive-driven little-house-at-the-center-of-the-universe type of town. You'll get used to it.

MIKE

Milwaukee is a city.

GARY

And New York is THE city—the only city to a lot of people out there. The best. The creme de la creme. The one place on earth where speed and agility count as much as talent. New Yorkers never stop moving. Not to eat. Not to sleep. Not to think and certainly not to pee. Running ten miles a day should help.

MIKE

I'll adjust.

GARY

I'm glad. Somebody has to . . . (*pause*) Just be careful. To the blest, this is paradise . . . to the rest of us, it's Potter's Field. That's why I'm leaving. I am a native and I am abandoning this good ship. Part of me isn't quite used to the idea, yet. But, I'll make the change. I'm determined. I'll adjust . . . too.

MIKE

You can always come back.

GARY

When you're gone . . . you're gone. (*quietly*) Poof! (*pause*)
Look . . . you have a lot of work to do—moving's a hassle—
if you don't mind, I'll give you a hand.

MIKE

Well . . .

GARY

I'd like to. Besides, I can tell you all about the building . . .
and you can use the help.

MIKE

(*uncertain*) If you really don't mind . . .

GARY

No problem. Let's go.

MIKE

Dressed like that?

GARY

Start adjusting. New Yorkers look different, too!

MIKE

Do they use the same money!

GARY

A joke! Wonderful!

(*They exit*)
(*Fade out.*)

SCENE TWO

(*The same. Mike is in the living room. Gary is [off] in the kitchen*)

GARY

[*off*] Make yourself comfortable. Sit down.

MIKE

I will. Thanks.

(*He looks around the apartment.*)

GARY

[*off*] I'll find the wine and be right out. What do you prefer —red or white? Hold on! Here it is!

MIKE

Red.

GARY

[*off*] How flexible are you?

MIKE

White is fine.

GARY

Good. (*enters*) I found the rose. Think of it as a mixture of both.

MIKE

Whatever you have . . . just tell me why you're keeping *crabs* in the livingroom.

GARY

You don't believe the line about handicapped pets?

MIKE

No.

GARY

(*shrugs*) I'm planning one last bash—a sort of "beat-the-marshal-to-the-door" eviction party. I hope it gives our drunken super a stroke! But anyway, I felt the party needed a theme—writer's love themes—so I decided to transform this dreary old dump into a stretch of beach very much removed from here and very near Papeete.

MIKE

Tahiti!

GARY

(*excited*) You've been there!

MIKE

No. I've never been further west than the Milwaukee public library. I spent some time there reading about Gauguin. I love his works.

GARY

I love his subject. With any luck, I'll spend eternity on those beaches.

MIKE

It would be a nice place to visit. It certainly seems beautiful.

GARY

I hope to stay.

MIKE

Then, I hope you get there. (*raises glass*) I give you "Tahiti".

GARY

I accept.

(*They drink. Long pause*)

But, for the moment, I am very much a prisoner of the present. This is the best I could do.

MIKE

It's quite a lot actually. Cleaning up won't be easy.

GARY

I am leaving that to the prince of darkness. You'll find him behind your door on the first of the month and lose him whenever anything breaks down. The sand alone should drive him nuts! The thought of him shovelling it all up and doing god knows what with it gave me incredible strength. There are seventy-three buckets of the stuff scattered all over the place—each one carried up here . . . with the help of the subway . . . all the way from Coney Island!

MIKE

You certainly take your parties seriously.

GARY

I have to. It's the last one. (*slight pause*) You're invited.

MIKE

I can't. I hardly know you.

GARY

It doesn't matter . . . I'm leaving, anyway. If you don't like me . . . (*shrugs*) Besides, I have two dozen crabs, a kitchen full of food, some incredibly potent Polynesian drink recipes and some other goodies buried all over this place. The more we finish—the less we leave behind. And, that goes for the wine, too! I've thrown away the cork.

MIKE

Then, I'll have to have another . . . and . . . I guess . . . I'll come! When is it?

GARY

Tonight.

MIKE

You're kidding?

GARY

Short notice is the best I can offer.

MIKE

We just met . . .

GARY

And the landlord takes possession tomorrow . . . one way or the other.

MIKE

But what about your stuff. You're not leaving it.

GARY

There is nothing left I value.

MIKE

Look . . . you helped me move in. I'll help you move out. It's the least I can do. Okay?

GARY

We'll see . . . in the morning. Right now . . . however . . . we have a party to consider. That is all I want to think about.

MIKE

Okay. When are the guests arriving?

GARY

Soon.

MIKE

Then I'd better hurry. I have to shower and change my clothes. These are filthy. I'll be right back.

GARY

Nonsense! You look fine. And, as for your clothes, this is Tahiti. I have costumes for everyone! (*He pulls a costume, similar to his, from a box*) You can change in the bathroom.

MIKE

Is this necessary?

GARY

It's part of the illusion. Go on. Change. (*Mike hesitates*) Think of Gauguin. You wouldn't want to appear *colonial*.

MIKE

Oh . . . what the hell!

(*He exits*)
(*Gary turns up the music. Looks around the room fondly. Someone bangs on the ceiling below. Gary strikes back with the hammer—as before.*)

GARY

Aloha, cocksucker! (*quietly*) Aloha
(*He picks up a crab. Speaks to it.*)
It won't be long now.
Soon.
Very soon.

(*Slow fade to black.*)

SCENE THREE

(*The same, only later. Gary and Mike have consumed most of the wine. No one else is present. Mike is still wearing his shirt with his costume.*)

MIKE

What time is it?

GARY

My friends are fashionably late. No one wants to be first.

MIKE

I was first.

GARY

I don't think they know about you.

(*Silence*)

MIKE

It's late, isn't it?

GARY

I don't know. I left my watch in New York.

MIKE

And I left mine in my other suit . . . which is . . . where?

GARY

Back in New York.

MIKE

Okay. But it is late.

GARY

You need another drink.

MIKE

Just a short one. To be sociable. What I really need is something to eat.

GARY

Shhhh! I don't want the crabs to hear! (*whispers*) A relaxed crab is a tender crab.

MIKE

(*whispering*) Oh . . . sorry.

GARY

I'll take them in the kitchen in a little while. It's too early to eat.

MIKE

(*after a pause*) You know . . . I didn't want to come . . .

GARY

You didn't have to . . . I mean . . . I didn't force you. I said, "You're invited". That's all. Not even a "please come".

MIKE

That's not what I meant. I didn't want to move . . .

GARY

I do.

MIKE

. . . to come HERE. It was the bosses idea. The promotion. More money. I didn't have to come. I don't *need* the money. But I couldn't say "no". Turn down a promotion . . . and they look at you funny. Where's your *ambition*. Can't you handle it? Can you handle it? They put you in a corner and they forget about you. They don't call on you again. They lose respect for you . . . for your ability . . . and then they lose you. Take the job . . . and you lose your home . . . everything familiar. (*pause*) I like my job.

GARY

What do ya do?

MIKE

I design the machines that make the plastic bags disposable diapers go in.

GARY

You're kidding.

MIKE

You have no idea . . . how big they are. I designed one that wouldn't fit in this room. Too big! And the only thing . . . the only thing . . . it does is make a plastic bag big enough to hold twenty-four little diapers. It does it faster an' cheaper than anything on earth.

GARY

I'm not very fast.

MIKE

All you have to do is push a button . . . one little, red button . . . and . . . vooooom! I made another machine . . . a bigger machine . . . that puts the diapers in the bag.

GARY

Fast.

MIKE

VOOOOM! What do you do?

GARY

I told you. I write . . . stories. I have this pen . . . a very special pen . . . I used it to create a whole new world.

MIKE

That's fantastic. Tell me about it.

GARY

It doesn't matter anymore. It was a long time ago and . . . well . . . no one gave a damn. (*shrugs*) It was a beautiful world.

MIKE

It's not your fault we already had a world.

GARY

That's a silly thing to say.

MIKE

No . . . no, it's not. My machine . . . there's only one like it. Nothing else works the same way. It's unique.

GARY

Mine was different. A totally unrestrained, passionately living, uninhibited society *is* unique!

MIKE

I'm not arguing with you.

GARY

(*getting a shoe box*) Do you know what this is?

MIKE

Confetti?

GARY

This is the sum total of every correspondence sent by me and every patronizing, frigid, form-framed rejection returned by *them* . . . chopped and mixed into one great indistinguishable, unintelligible mass. There is a blizzard in this box . . . a blizzard I hope to return *by the fistful* . . . when I leave. (*tosses handful*) Bon Voyage! You bastards! I'm taking my world. I'm heading for *Tahiti*. I'm . . . I'm . . . HELL . . . I am going to try it!

MIKE

You'll make it.

GARY

Promise?

MIKE

What . . . sure . . .

GARY

Thanks!

MIKE

I'm sorry they didn't like your book.

GARY

It doesn't matter. I'd like a drink.

MIKE

I'll pour.

GARY

You are a gentleman.

MIKE

I've been giving this a lot of thought. Tomorrow—after the party, after your friends leave—we'll move all your stuff into my apartment. *You can stay with me!* We'll take everything downstairs and lock this place. And leave it! When the marshall comes, he can have what's left.

GARY

What's that?

MIKE

SAND! Let him have it all!

GARY

You're drunk.

MIKE

That's right.

GARY

In the morning . . . you won't mean it.

MIKE

I've got plenty of room . . . and you seem like a nice guy. You're crazy—but I can get used to that. You need a place to stay. I have a place. And, I'm sober enough to remember everything I just said . . . when the time comes.

GARY

You're nice to offer. But, I have a place . . . and a plan.

MIKE

You sure.

GARY

Yes. (*pause*) Take my furniture when I'm gone.

MIKE

I don't want your furniture!

GARY

The super will take it . . . if you don't. And, I hate him.

MIKE

I'll save it for you.

GARY

Do whatever you want.

MIKE

I want a drink.

GARY

(*pouring*) The bar's open.

MIKE

What time is it?

GARY

It doesn't matter.

(*Fade to black. End: Scene Three.*)

SCENE FOUR

(The same. Later still. And, drunker still.)

MIKE

Your party is dying.

GARY

I'm sorry.

MIKE

No . . . I'm having a good . . . a great time!

GARY

Then it's okay.

MIKE

Your friends . . . aren't here.

GARY

Then they're missing a good party.

MIKE

One hell of a party. Can we eat now?

GARY

Shhhh!

MIKE

Sorry. It must be late by now.

GARY

Yup.

MIKE

I thought so. I gotta go to the bathroom.

GARY

Be my guest.

(*Mike gets up, stumbles and knocks an ashtray off the table.*)

MIKE

Ooops! (*pounding from below*) Uh-oh! You've got mice!

GARY

I'll get 'em. (*bangs with hammer*) Take that . . . you vermin!

MIKE

I'll be right back.

GARY

I'll pour you a drink.

MIKE

Are you trying to get me drunk?

GARY

Yup.

MIKE

It's . . . not . . . working. (*lurches off*)

(*Gary seems to sober somewhat. He is obviously high, but in control. He pours two drinks. In Mike's, he adds a pill. Then, he goes to his desk, removes a sealed envelope, writes on it and carefully places it on top of the shoe box. He seems satisfied.*)
(*Mike re-enters*)

GARY

(*handing him his "drink"*) I'd like to propose a toast.

MIKE

Here-here!

GARY

To necessary friends.

MIKE

Your friends aren't here.

GARY

You're here. Are you my friend?

MIKE

I'd like to be.

GARY

Then, drink up. Don't be rude.

MIKE

To necessary friends. Cheers!

(*He downs the drink. Gary does not drink.*)

GARY

(*sounding less drunk; almost sober*) Good. (*takes him by the hand*) Now, sit down. You're drunk. I don't want you to fall. Please . . . sit.

MIKE

(*sitting heavily*) It's your party.

GARY

Thank you.

MIKE

Now what?

GARY

Nothing. Just relax and listen. Okay? (*Mike nods. Pause*) I don't know how to begin . . . this part I didn't plan. (*pause*) My friends aren't coming. I didn't invite any of them. And . . . even if I wanted them here . . . most would have been busy. We've all changed too much over the years. They've gotten what they wanted . . . most of what they wanted. They don't understand anymore, I'm just the crazy one of the bunch. (*pause*) I thought about this party for a long time. I planned it over a year ago. I knew I'd have to move . . . I'd have to force a change. That's when I decided to be alone tonight. You see, I told them about my magic pen and the wholy new, completely different world I created. I listened to them talk about their new homes and new cars, their stocks, their bonds, their *taxes,* the cost of private school, the cost of mink, the cost of gold, the cost of this and that and how much cheaper this and that was in Europe . . . or in Mexico. I listened to their world and told them about mine and knew . . . knew . . . they weren't interested at all. Not one of them asked to read my book. One by one I crossed them off my guest list. And, when I was finally ready, when time and circumstances brought me to this moment, I thought I would be alone. I'm glad you moved into this building. You've made it easier. (*Gary takes a pill*) Mike, I want you to listen to me very carefully. Can you understand what I'm saying?

MIKE

(*with difficulty*) What . . . was . . . that . . .

GARY

A pill . . . something I have to take. Will you listen to me?

MIKE

I . . . don't . . . feel . . . so . . . good . . .

GARY

I know. You have to listen. Okay? (*Mike nods*) There is a note by the phone. I want you to read it when you wake up. I put something in your drink . . . to make you sleep. It won't hurt you . . . it's not the pill I took. You'll sleep. That's all. I want you to remember to read the note.

MIKE

What . . . did . . . you . . . take . . .

(*Gary crosses to a chair and sits.*)

GARY

(*matter-of-fact*) Poison.

MIKE

I'll . . . call . . . a . . . doctor . . .

(*He tries to get up. It is too late. He falls back, struggles briefly and sleeps.*)

GARY

Please don't. (*closes eyes*) Aloha!

(*Slow blackout.*)

EPILOGUE

(The same—the following morning. Gary, still in the chair, is dead.)

MIKE

Gary . . . this isn't funny.

(long pause)

Come on . . . Gary . . . wake up. It's morning. We have to move your stuff. Okay?

(long pause)

Talk to me, damnit! Tell me this whole thing was a joke. I'll understand. This hangover I've got . . . the throbbing, the pain . . . it was just too much booze. Nothing else. We both had a good time . . . it was a good party and . . . we drank too much . . . that's all. Tell me! I'll laugh. I promise.

(long pause)

You had no right—not to involve me this way. I don't know you . . . hell, I just got off a bus from . . . what the hell am I supposed to do . . . you son-of-a-bitch! You got me into this —now what? *(to himself)* I've got to get help. I've . . . *(to Gary)* I'm going to call the police, and then I'm leaving. You got that, Gary? *No more!*

(He goes to the phone and picks it up before seeing the note)

I am not reading this. I remember what you said. I don't care. I am turning you . . . and your damn suicide note . . . over to the police. That's it. GOOD BYE!

(*He slams the receiver down*)

SHIT!

(*Mike sits. He is very quiet.*)

You shouldn't have done this. (*he opens the letter. Reads.*) "I am Gary Evan Sloane. This is my last will and testament . . ." Oh, god! "I leave everything I own to whomever finds me. I realize it isn't worth much. There is, however, one item I cherish. It has been good to me. In the desk, you will find an old, red fountain pen. Please keep it. Take care of it. I have made most of the arrangements for my death. I wish to be cremated. The necessary papers are also in the desk. I have but one request. It is my last wish, the one I could not arrange in advance. It is up to you. I wish to be set to rest on the beach in Tahiti. Please sprinkle my ashes on the sand. I trust, I have to trust, that you will help me. If, for some reason, however, you cannot go to Tahiti, do me a smaller favor. Pay the postage. Deliver me to paradise. Thank you."

(*long pause*)

You were a crazy son-of-a . . .

(*He picks up the phone. Pause. He sets the receiver down gently on the desk top. He opens the desk drawer and finds the pen. He rolls it around in his fingers and looks at Gary.*)

A crazy son-of-a-bitch.

(*Mike puts the pen in his shirt pocket. He nods at Gary, then dials the phone.*)
(*Slow blackout.*)

The End